ng

Parenting a Grieving Child

Helping Children

Find Faith,

Hope,

and Healing

after the Loss of a

Loved One

MARY DeTURRIS POUST

LOYOLAPRESS.

CHICAGO

LOYOLAPRESS.

3441 N. ASHLAND AVENUE
CHICAGO, ILLINOIS 60657

Interior design by Eileen Wagner
Cover image © Digital Stock Corp.

Library of Congress Cataloging-in-Publication Data
Poust, Mary DeTurris.
Parenting a grieving child: helping children find faith, hope, and healing after the
loss of a loved one / Mary DeTurris Poust.
p. cm.
ISBN 0-8294-1527-0
1. Bereavement in children—Religious aspects—Christianity. 2. Parenting—
Religious aspects—Christianity. 3. Children and death—Religious aspects—
Christianity. I. Title.

BV4596.P3 P68 2002
248.8'66—dc21   2001050590

Printed in the United States of America
02 03 04 05 Bang 10 9 8 7 6 5 4 3 2 1

To my mother, Irene DeTurris,
whose absence I will mourn and
whose life I will celebrate
all of my days.

And to my husband, Dennis,
and our children, Noah and Olivia,
whose love and enthusiasm
fill me with joy
and make my life complete.

Contents

3.

A Shoulder to Lean On: Supporting Our Children As They Deal with Their Emotions

4.

Gone Forever: Helping Children Adjust to Permanent Loss

5.

When the Time Is Right: Learning to Start Over

6.

When the Unthinkable Happens: Guiding
Our Children through Traumatic Loss

7.

Watch, Listen, and Learn: Respecting
Our Children's Grief

8.

9.

Acknowledgments

There is only one place to begin, and that is with my husband, Dennis. From the moment I expressed my desire to write this book, he has been my rock, my cheerleader, my first line editor, and the best friend and partner I could ever hope for. He read every page of this manuscript as it came rolling off my printer and offered insights and suggestions that have made this book so much better than it otherwise would have been.

Our children, Noah James and Olivia Irene, are really too young to know what all this means, but I have to thank them anyway for their patience and their willingness to put up with Mommy's crazy schedule. There were many sunny days when we had to forgo the park so that I could finish another chapter or conduct one more interview. They were troopers, even if they didn't always suffer in silence.

The list of people who helped make this book a reality is almost endless. First, I want to thank my friend David Scott, who believed in this project and pushed me to make it happen. And then there is Jim Manney, my editor at Loyola Press, who enthusiastically supported this book through proposals, outlines, writing, and editing. His encouragement and suggestions gave me confidence in my subject and in my ability to turn an idea into a manuscript. A special thank-you goes to Evelyn Bence, another editor whose insights and ideas helped me immensely.

I would also like to thank my aunt Margaret Robertson, whose expertise as a teacher and experience as a mother played a significant role in the development of the activities included in each chapter. In addition, she and my cousin Brendan provided invaluable baby-sitting assistance when I was in the final stages of finishing this manuscript.

I could not have written this book without the many wonderful people who opened their hearts and shared their stories with me. Most of them never even met me, yet they talked with me for hours on the phone, sent me e-mails, wrote me notes, and made me cry with their honesty, their faith, and their determination to go on despite the incredible burdens they have been asked to bear. They touched my life and reminded me to savor every day I have with the people I love.

Finally, I would like to thank my family—my father and stepmother, my brother and sister, my grandmother, my aunts, my uncles, and my cousins—from Pearl River, New York, to Pflugerville, Texas. They have supported me by being excited about this book and by always having faith in me, no matter what I endeavor to do. Thank you.

Introduction

> I will turn their mourning into joy,
>   I will console and gladden them after
> their sorrows.
>
> Jeremiah 31:13

Sometimes I try to imagine what my children's lives would be like without me. How would they remember me—if they could remember me at all? Would they know my voice, my face, the fact that I love them with a force more powerful than gravity? It's an infrequent but excruciating little exercise that makes me hug them more and yell at them less. Maybe it sounds morbid or crazy, but the reality is that plenty of children do know the sorrow of losing a parent, a sibling, a grandparent, or a friend.

Unfortunately, we are all experts when it comes to grief. At some point or another, we all know the meaning of loneliness and fear. We wake up and wonder how we will get out of bed, face another day, take another breath. Losing someone you love can be like that. To know that we are helpless to protect our children from such sorrow has got to be one of parenthood's greatest frustrations.

But we parents can learn from each other, from our children, and from those who shared their darkest fears and deepest sorrows for the creation of this book.

In these pages, you will find stories of real parents who helped their children cope with death. You will hear advice from doctors, therapists, funeral directors, chaplains, and others who have witnessed the powerful process that death sets in motion for those left behind. You will discover that if you are willing to take that first step on the road through grief and mourning, hope and life do win out in the end.

You can begin this book at chapter 1 and read it all the way through, or you can open it to whichever chapter most suits your needs and begin reading there. I hope it will be a manual, a reference book, a guide, and a comfort as you struggle to help your children understand death, which our faith allows us to view as another part of life.

When I began writing this book, I was sure I would find a lot of hard-and-fast rules about helping children grieve. I assumed that children would act in very specific ways, depending on the loss they had suffered. I couldn't have been more wrong. What I learned instead is that every child—just like every adult—grieves on his or her own terms. Personalities, family dynamics, relationships, spirituality: these same things that make each one of us an individual also allow each one of us to grieve in a unique way.

If there is a universal truth regarding children and grief it is that we parents must be prepared for and open to a wide range of reactions from our children. We may not understand or approve, but we can try to find ways to be nonjudgmental and supportive so that our children will feel comfortable grieving on their own terms.

This book is not just for those whose children are in the throes of grief. This book is also for parents and other adults who realize that someday the children in their lives will face loss and heartache and sadness. This book is for anyone who has ever wondered how to talk to a child about death or whether to talk about death at all. This book is for all of us who want to know what to say and how to listen. And this book is for every child who has known the kind of sorrow that parents dare to imagine only in their worst nightmares.

1

It's Their Loss, Too: Letting Children Grieve

- **What is your first death memory?**

- **Is one loss worse than another?**

- **How much does it hurt?**

- **How can our own memories help our children?**

- **Where does faith fit in?**

- **What's the difference between grief and mourning?**

When someone you care about dies, it's very sad. There will be tears, but tears can be good.
Michaelene Mundy, *Sad Isn't Bad*

I was only five years old when my grandfather died of a heart attack in a local bowling alley. I remember that October day like it was yesterday. I can see myself sitting in the backseat of my grandmother's big white car as she drove up to the front of her house, only to find a priest and the next-door neighbors waiting outside on the porch. It's a wonderfully vivid memory. Unfortunately, none of it is true. It is the creation of a child's imagination, an imagination that was left to make its own memories when there wasn't enough reality to explain the confusion and sadness all around.

My grandfather's death was a mystery to me. One day he was there—pushing me in my swing in the willow tree in his backyard, teasing me relentlessly as we ate lunch together, convincing me that the booming thunder that sent me running to his big, brown armchair was God bowling in the attic. The next day he was gone. No one gave me any details. No one told me what was happening. All I knew was that now when I knelt down to say my prayers before bed, I asked God to bless Grandpa in heaven, instead of plain old Grandpa.

But heaven can be a pretty hard concept to grasp, especially when you're five years old and the only loss you've experienced is watching your best friend move away. I didn't know where heaven was or what it meant that my grandfather was going there. Since I wasn't allowed to attend his wake or funeral, I never really understood that he was gone for good. For a couple of years after his death, I expected him to show up in church on Sunday. I knew that my family had gone there to say good-bye, so it seemed only logical that he would return there eventually.

It wasn't until I was old enough to realize that the big, gray stone at the cemetery, the one engraved with praying hands and my last name, was his grave. I was seven years old when it finally dawned on me that Grandpa wasn't coming back on Sunday morning or any other day.

When my own mother died of cancer twenty years later, my aunt asked me if she should allow my five-year-old cousin to attend the wake and funeral. I told her about my experience and encouraged her to let him go if that was what he wanted. The result was truly an eye-opener for me. Not only did Gregory want to go to the wake, he actually ended up being a comfort to the adults around him.

I remember how he bravely walked up to the casket with my Aunt Margaret at his side. He looked at my mother and told my tearful aunt, "Don't cry, Mommy. Aunt Irene is happy now." It was all the proof I needed to convince me that children cannot be separated from the grieving process. They are aware of the sadness and mourning around them when someone dies, and they need to understand the reason for that sadness if they are ever going to move beyond it and begin to heal.

Although I had put all of those family memories on the shelf for quite some time, I had always wanted to explore them more thoroughly and find a way to help parents walk their children through the rocky terrain of death, grief, and mourning. That is how this book was born.

cℐℴ

What is your first death memory?

When was the first time you were exposed to death? Was it a friend, a relative, someone who was part of your daily life, or a distant uncle you hardly knew?

For some children it is the loss of a sibling that turns life upside down. For others it is the death of an aged grandparent, an ill parent, a beloved friend, or a faithful pet. Children are deeply affected by the death of a loved one, regardless of who it is or how it happens. Although different kinds of deaths may cause different kinds of reactions, no loss is ever easy. Depending on a child's age and the kind of relationship she had with the deceased, grief reactions can range from mild sadness to physical illness to powerful shifts toward aggressive behavior or complete withdrawal. Any loss can be a major loss to a child.

Although I never said a word to my parents, as a child I secretly wondered about my grandfather's disappearance from my life. I overheard stories that scared me and fed my imagination. There were tales of relatives fainting at the wake, of smelling salts, of endless crying. There was the long mourning period, which I don't remember but which surely had an impact. How many afternoons can a five-year-old sit at her grandmother's house with no radio, no television, and no laughter? My sister, who was only six months old when our grandfather died, cried every time someone sang "Happy Birthday" well into her childhood. As best we can guess, it came from seeing our family members crying at every birthday and holiday celebration in the years after Grandpa's death.

My first experience with death influenced all of my subsequent experiences with death and the way I now handle the subject with my own children. I already talk to my son about death more often than I ever imagined I would. It seems that almost every movie and every book presents an opportunity to talk about death, or at least about life. And despite how it appears on the surface, that's not a bad thing.

Is one loss worse than another?

We may assume there is some sort of hierarchy of grieving scenarios. Is it worse to lose a parent than a grandparent? Is it more painful to lose a sibling to a car accident than to leukemia? The reality is that whatever loss a child is grieving it is the worst possible loss that child can fathom. It does not matter that it was the expected death of a girl's ninety-five-year-old grandma. It is still the death of a beloved friend who used to tell her stories in the afternoon.

Donna Schuurman, executive director of the Dougy Center, a grief support program in Portland, Oregon, says that comparisons don't come into play when a child is grieving. What matters is the relationship the child had with the deceased person. "If that grandparent was really instrumental in her life, she's not going to think, 'Old people die. It's better than losing my sixteen-year-old friend.' She's going to think, 'I've lost someone in my life who is not going to be there anymore—and that hurts.' It doesn't become a comparative process. The worst loss is the one you are experiencing."

That same philosophy applies when it comes to the way a loved one dies. A judgment of better or worse just doesn't matter when we're talking about life and death. Is sudden death by car accident, for example, somehow worse for a child to deal with than the loss of a loved one due to an extended illness? Yes, there can be an incompleteness when someone dies suddenly. There are no opportunities to say good-bye, to end an argument, to say what needs to be said. On the other hand, although long-term illness provides an opportunity to prepare for the death, it can also bring other hardships for the survivors. People often don't look like themselves after an extended illness. They may even lose their mental capabilities, making it especially difficult for children to cope.

"It doesn't really matter how the loved one died," says Schuurman. "Imagine saying to a kid, 'At least your father died of cancer and not in a car accident.' What point does that make? You can actually have a kid whose father dies of suicide and a kid whose father dies in a car accident, and the one who's dealing with the suicide is doing much better."

So how do we know how badly our children are hurting? For one thing, we need to be open to the possibility that they may be grieving deeply over a loss that we consider fairly insignificant. We are all impacted by death in very different ways. When was the last time you looked at the obituary page and stopped to read about the life and death of someone you never even met? Death moves us. Death scares us. Death makes us think about all the what-ifs.

Our children may not approach death in such a conscious way, but they do take in the seriousness of what is happening around them, even though they often do so in thoroughly selfish ways.

A child who loses a parent will typically run through a laundry list of self-centered questions: How will this affect me? What happens now? Am I going to be able to go to college? Who's going to teach me how to drive? Will I ever be able to go camping again? It isn't until later that the child will start to notice more significant things, like the fact that her father, who died at age forty-two, won't ever get to experience the rest of his life, that he lost out on the chance to raise his children, grow old with his wife, achieve his career goals, meet his grandchildren. So we have to meet our children where they are, even if where they are seems remarkably self-absorbed and not at all what we expect of someone in grief.

How much does it hurt?

While every loss impacts a child in a meaningful way, there is
no doubt that certain losses can impact a child in devastating
ways. We can talk about the uniqueness of every child. We
can even talk about the fact that one child may handle the loss
of a parent better than another handles the loss of a friend.
But the bottom line is that some deaths have the power to
incapacitate our children.

For children who live at home with their parents and
siblings, the loss of a mother, father, brother, or sister is about
as devastating as it gets. Having lost my own mother when I
was twenty-five years old, I can assure anyone who has never
lost a parent that this was about as painful an experience as I
could ever imagine at that point in my life.

She was my mother, after all, but she was also much
more than that. She was my confidant, my best friend, and
my hero. I could not imagine my life without her. There
were many times not long after her death when I picked up
the phone to call her with some news about my job or just
to say hello. There were many times I tried to look into
the future and imagine how I would get through all those
years filled with holidays and happiness, new babies and new
homes, sickness and sorrow without my mother to lean on.
As is almost always the case, we do get through, and we
get stronger, but it is not easy.

Imagine how overwhelming it must be for a young child
to face life without a mother or father, to look down that long

road of elementary school, high school, college, and beyond and see the empty space where a parent should be. There is a bond between most parents and children that runs far deeper than any other bond we encounter in our lifetimes.

Of course there are exceptions to every rule, and for some children, the loss of a parent may not be the most difficult loss they will face. If a boy hasn't seen his father in six years, the father's death is going to have a very different impact than if his father had been living with him. By the same token, if a girl's grandfather was her main father figure, the death of her grandfather will be a monumental loss.

The same can hold true for aunts, uncles, cousins, and friends. Those who have key roles in a child's life, serving as mentors, friends, protectors, and surrogate parents, will be missed more deeply than those who have had only a passing acquaintance with the child. It is not always a matter of who was more loved but of who was more involved.

In most cases, losing a parent or a sibling will change the very fiber of a child's life. Mommy will no longer be there to walk him to school, to pack his favorite lunch, to tuck him in at night. Or, in the case of a deceased sibling, the surviving child may mourn not only the loss of a sister, but also the loss of a roommate, a buddy, a sparring partner, and an ally. These losses cannot be stacked up and compared to the death of a grandparent who lives across the country or even a friend who lives down the street.

When it comes to dealing with our children and their grief, we parents must resist the urge to think like adults. We have

to get down on their level, like we do when they're a year old
and we're childproofing the house. Look at the death from
your child's perspective. Think about the relationship your
child had with the person who has died. Remember the way
the death occurred and how that might be affecting your child.
Then, in a sense, toss all of it out the window and simply listen
to what your child is saying and watch what he or she is doing.

How can our own memories help our children?

If we are going to be helpful to our children, we need to
understand our own experiences with death. The beliefs we
have and the way our own grief and mourning were handled
by those around us all come into play as we try to deal with
our children's first confrontation with this difficult subject.

I didn't learn that my vivid recollections of my grandfather's death were false until I started doing the research for
this book. All those years I thought I had been there, a witness
to my grandmother's initial shock and grief, but I had never
stopped to verify it. That was due in part to the fact that talking
about death or about dead people was—and still is to some
degree—a taboo subject on the Italian side of my family. So I
took snippets of what people said and crafted my own story—
a common practice among children who do not get all of the
information they need.

When I made my first communion in second grade, I was
given a small pendant with a pair of praying hands on it, hands
that matched the ones on my grandfather's tombstone. For me,

that necklace became a kind of link. It reminded me of him, and that was all I needed to turn it into a keepsake of the time we spent together. Even now I keep a worn, pig-shaped cutting board on display in my kitchen because it reminds me of the lunches I shared with my grandfather. These little physical remembrances may not seem like much, but they are telltale signs of the power of loss in our lives. We want those around us to recognize our grief, and we want a way to keep the memory of our loved one alive.

What kind of memories does your first death experience stir up? If you think about them and reflect on them, they will serve as guideposts as you lead your own child down the road to healing.

Where does faith fit in?

For most of us, everything we think about life, death, and the afterlife is wrapped up in our religious beliefs. What we believe happens to us after we die can shape the way we react to death and the way we encourage our children to react to death. Before we can begin to use our faith to guide our children through grief and mourning, however, we must be clear and honest about our own feelings toward our faith and its teachings about death and resurrection.

A parent who is caught up in a blame game with God, accusing him of taking a loved one away as punishment for some action, will pass that belief on to a child. On the other hand, a parent who tries too hard to sugarcoat the image of heaven could end up creating equally confusing and potentially damaging problems.

Our faith teaches us that life never ends; it simply changes form. Often the death of a loved one can put that belief to the test. How we respond to the inevitable feelings of anger and doubt will influence how our children respond in similar situations. If we look at our faith in an honest and simple way, we can begin to translate the difficult concepts into something our children can understand.

We cannot separate our faith from our grief and mourning. They are delicately intertwined, and for most of us, that is a blessing. Talk to people who have suffered tragic losses, and time and again they will say that they could not have made it through the difficult times had it not been for their faith. Even when they are angry at God and wondering about the wisdom of his will, they are still connected to a powerful belief system that helps them make sense of the confusion.

I was a senior in high school when my grandmother was hit by a car while crossing a busy road in my hometown. We prayed to God, Mary, and every saint whose name had ever crossed our consciousness. She died five years after the accident, having never recovered physically or mentally. At that point in my life, I was filled with faith. In fact, my mother and I had been returning from a youth group outing to see Pope John Paul II at Madison Square Garden in New York City on the day my grandmother was hit. Our bus passed the accident on the way back into town, but we had no idea how that scene would impact our lives. Throughout my grandmother's ordeal, I prayed. We all prayed, and we used our faith like a life preserver to keep us afloat in a stormy sea.

When my mother was diagnosed with cancer a few years later, I convinced myself that God would not take her. After all, he took my grandmother too young and too tragically. Surely he was not going to come knocking again so soon at my family's door. I'm not sure where that idea came from, thinking that God was keeping some kind of life and death tally. Maybe it was just a way to ward off the inevitable. The Sunday before my mother died was the first time in my life that I chose to skip Mass. I was trying to stare down God in a fight for my mother's life, and going to church while he let her die in our family room would have been like blinking first, or so I thought at the time.

When God—and death—did come for my mother early in the morning on April 12, I was not so filled with faith. I was filled with rage, disbelief, despair, and hopelessness. At that moment in my life, faith seemed far out of reach.

Death forces us to look more closely at our faith and at how much we believe or don't believe. The night before my mother died, as we stood around her bed while our parish priest gave her the sacrament of the sick, my mother's father stood on the sidelines. He was adamant that she did not need the anointing, that she was going to be cured. He prayed his novena, not asking God to spare her life but asking that God's will be done. When my mother died the next morning, my grandfather did not lose faith. He may have been in anguish over his daughter's death, but he held fast to the belief that

God does answer every prayer, just not always with the answer we want when we send up our request.

So, wherever we are in our faith journey will play a starring role in our grief journey. The two become one, and with wisdom and courage, the two can make us whole again. That wholeness will help us to comfort and guide our grieving children.

What's the difference between grief and mourning?

What do those two terms—*grief* and *mourning*—mean for us and for our children? Grief is the emotional stress caused by death, loss, or other traumatic events in our lives. Mourning is the way we outwardly display that grief. While those definitions sound neat and clean, remember that when we're talking about our emotional lives, things are never that easy. Life is a roller coaster of feelings.

Every grieving child, regardless of age, and every grieving adult for that matter, must move through a series of stages known as tasks: We accept the reality of loss; we allow ourselves to feel the feelings that come with loss; we adjust to life without our loved one; and we invest in new relationships and move on with life.

The tasks represent our human response to grief and our effort to pull ourselves through it. They allow us to get through our grief and mourning to a place where the loss we have suffered has been integrated into our lives in a healthy way. If we don't deal with issues that are simmering below the surface, we set the stage for potential problems that could linger for years. For children, getting caught in these unresolved tasks can spell developmental disaster that reaches well into adulthood.

THINGS TO REMEMBER

It can be hard for us parents to watch as a child deals with grief. We want the child to feel better, to return to "normal" as soon as possible. It helps if we can remember that, when it comes to grieving, "normal" takes on a whole new meaning.

DON'T GET INTO COMPARISONS. One death is not worse than or better than another. Even the death of a goldfish can be a huge loss for a child.

BE COMPASSIONATE and allow your child to feel sad or angry.

DON'T BE FOOLED BY OUTWARD BEHAVIOR. Children sometimes appear unaffected by loss, but the reality is that their grief will come out at some point. You can help it along by being available to your child—to listen, to play, to cry, to pray.

ASK SIMPLE QUESTIONS or make simple statements that help your child articulate his own feelings:
- "It sure is quiet around the house without Spot's barking. I miss him."
- "How are you feeling today? Do you want to go for a walk with me?"

In the chapters that follow, we will explore these tasks in depth, looking at how they are manifested in a child's life and how we can encourage our children to work through each one, no matter their age or developmental stage. Together we will discover why kids need to grieve.

- "This was Grandma's favorite [song, season, food, sweater, etc.]. Remember when [recall a specific event here]?"
- "Would you like to keep this [book, doll, necklace, etc.] as a reminder of your sister?"

LET YOUR CHILD SEE YOUR OWN GRIEF. Don't be afraid to be sad together.

SAY A FAVORITE PRAYER TOGETHER or make something up as you go along. You can use the prayer below as a guide.

Dear God,
Losing someone we love
is like losing a part of ourselves.
It hurts inside and makes us sad.
Give us the strength and the courage
to face each day with hope
in your promise of heaven.
Lift up our spirits and
heal our broken hearts.
Amen.

ACTIVITY

From Caterpillar to Butterfly: Talking about Resurrection

It's hard for kids to grasp the concept of resurrection, so it helps if we can find a way to put this complex subject into simple terms. Here's one way to talk about resurrection to younger children.

STEP 1. Read the story "Waiting for Wings" by Lois Ehlert (or some other butterfly book that may be a favorite of your child's), and talk about how the caterpillar was transformed into a butterfly after a short time in its cocoon. Reflect on the fact that the butterfly is not a different creature but the same caterpillar given a new kind of life. Help your child to see the original caterpillar in the transformed butterfly.

STEP 2. Talk about how the transformation of our loved one from death to resurrection is similar to the caterpillar's transformation. When we die we are transformed by God into new creations. We are the same but different. Just like the caterpillar, we are given a new life—eternity with God in heaven.

STEP 3. Help your child create a caterpillar-butterfly to illustrate the concept:

- Take a cardboard tube from a roll of paper towels and paint it or cover it with contact paper or fabric. Add stickers, glitter, drawings, or any other designs.

ACTIVITY

- Take two pipe cleaners and glue them onto one end of the tube for antennae. Curl the ends up or glue small pom-poms to the ends. Now you have a caterpillar.
- Next, fold a piece of colored construction paper in half. Draw the outline of a wing on one half. Cut the folded paper so that when you open it the wings are symmetrical.
- Open the wings and let your child paint on one side only. Tell him to close the wings over and press the two sides together so that the painting creates a symmetrical design. Let the wings dry.
- Wrap the caterpillar in tissue, gauze, or even a towel. Explain to your child that the caterpillar is in its cocoon.
- The next day (or however long you'd like to wait —three days, perhaps), take the caterpillar out of its cocoon and glue it into the crease of the wings. The caterpillar has been transformed into a beautiful butterfly.

2

What Children Need to Know: Explaining Death and Dying

- **How do we help children grasp the reality of loss?**

- **What *does* it mean when you die?**

- **How much do children really understand?**

- **How can we talk with our children about death?**

- **How do we manage that first good-bye?**

My job was to lead the children through these moments—to press but not too hard.

Gregory Floyd, *A Grief Unveiled*

My son and I were coming out of the bookstore one morning when we almost stepped on a tiny brown sparrow that was lying motionless on the sidewalk. We stopped, and Noah looked up at me with his big brown eyes as if to say, "Do something." I knelt down next to him and told him that the bird couldn't fly anymore, that his heart wasn't beating. He looked at me again and said, "The birdie is sleeping." I held his hand and, despite that agreeing with his sleep theory would have provided a nice way out of a lot more questions and confusion, I told him, "No, the birdie is dead. He's not breathing. He's not going to wake up." Later that night, when we were sitting around the dinner table, I asked Noah if he wanted to tell his father about his day. He reported on our trip to the bookstore and our discovery outside. Then he said quite matter-of-factly, "The birdie is sad." That was it. Somehow his two-and-a-half-year-old mind took what I was saying and translated it into something he could understand. No more flying, no more breathing, no more chirping. The birdie must be sad. It was his first brush with death, an experience that I hope on some level will prepare him for whatever more difficult losses come next.

⌒∽

Ask a child what it means to be dead, and you're likely to get answers that will surprise and shock you. While some children seem to have a firm grasp on the concept and may even sound philosophical, others may be locked into a kind of magical thinking that leaves them scared, guilty, and unable to move beyond the initial and intense stages of grief.

Children of different ages and developmental stages perceive death in different ways. A very young infant may understand only that something is upsetting his otherwise secure and happy environment. A teenager, on the other hand, may be overwhelmed by her understanding of the finality of death and her unwillingness to acknowledge her own mortality. Every age group in between has its own worries, confusions, beliefs, and reactions to losses that are suffered along the way—whether it's the family pet that dies in the yard one night, an older sibling who is killed in a tragic accident, or a beloved grandparent who finally succumbs to a hard-fought battle with disease.

How do we help children grasp the reality of loss?

Jennifer Morgan remembers with vivid detail what it was like to learn that her fourteen-year-old brother had died. Although it happened more than fifteen years ago, the memories are still fresh.

"I was ten years old when Robby died. He drowned on a Boy Scout trip. It was Memorial Day weekend. What a tragedy. I remember it like it was yesterday. He was in the kitchen making potato pancakes, and I was on my way to a friend's birthday slumber party. He was leaving the next morning, and I kissed him good-bye. That was the last time I saw my big brother."

She remembers being at the local ball field for a softball game when word came that there had been an accident. She and her younger brother and sister were taken to a friend's house. They waited there for hours before they were driven back to their own home, where friends and neighbors had gathered to comfort their parents.

"I walked in and saw my mom sitting in a chair crying. I was so confused. What happened? Our friend who is a priest approached us and told us that Robby was in heaven. How could that be? I didn't get it. He was supposed to be in Delaware. From then on my life would never be the same."

So often we parents and other adults assume that children do not need to grieve. We try to protect them from the sadness and the hurt. We send them away to stay with distant relatives. We ignore their questions in hopes that the curiosity will disappear on its own. Sometimes we even tell them stories that do more harm than good.

Like young Jennifer, who could not understand how her brother could be in heaven when he was supposed to be in Delaware, children who lose a loved one must first come to understand the reality of what has happened before they can even begin to grieve. It is up to us parents to help them make sense of the chaos and to give them the basic information they need to process the event.

"I remember it like it was yesterday, telling the kids about Robby's death," says Lorraine Wilson, Jennifer's mother. "They related to heaven. They had a belief in God. We told them that Robby was not coming home. It was like telling a story. It didn't seem like we were telling them about our son, about Robby."

But telling them the truth was the best thing the Wilsons could have done for their children. The reality was that Robby was never coming home, and if his siblings were going to accept that and begin to grieve and mourn, they had to know the truth.

We don't have to give children gory details of injuries or circumstances, and we shouldn't use confusing euphemisms for death. We do have to give them the real story, even if it is an abridged version. We can say, "It was a car accident," instead of saying, "Dad went to sleep and didn't wake up." According to experts, 99 percent of the time our children know the real story even when we think we are shielding them from it. By not telling or bending the truth, we are breaking a trust between our children and ourselves at a critical time in their lives.

We start with honesty and move out from there. Perhaps we can encourage our children to draw a picture or write a poem about what they are feeling. For those children who aren't ready to express themselves in such open ways, we can offer them opportunities to bare their souls through dolls and puppets or even physical activity.

As always, the best way to teach our children how to grieve is to show them by example. We can sit down with a photo album of our loved one and talk about that person's favorite places, the things he said, the dreams she had. We can let our children see our own weakness and sadness in the face of sorrow and, at the same time, our own strength and faith.

What *does* it mean when you die?

Depending on a child's age, death can mean different things. As children journey through the various stages of growing up, they learn to put abstract ideas into a framework that they can wrap their minds around. They use the tools with which they are most comfortable. A very young child may rely on the fantasy of fairy tales and cartoons to explain the loss of a loved one. A teen may withdraw even deeper inside himself in order to avoid the reality he knows is out there.

We parents can reflect on our children and where they are in those developmental stages before we start talking to them about death. How do our children deal with other problems in their lives? Do they have active imaginations that rely on magical ideas and fantastic stories? Are they moving beyond those early coping methods to perhaps a more realistic and concrete view of the world around them? Are they caught between childhood and adulthood in the difficult teen years, where they seem old enough to deal with adult concepts but actually are still children?

Often the best way to start this whole process is to sit back and listen to what our children are saying. If we are willing to open our ears and our hearts to their ways of thinking and seeing, chances are they will lead us exactly to where they need us to be. By listening and asking questions—not prying questions, but simple and direct questions—we can understand what our children need us to do for them.

In his book *Helping Children Cope with Grief,* Dr. Alan Wolfelt says that listening to our children requires us to hear not only the content of what they are saying but also the many things they are only hinting at.

"Take your time and patiently listen to your child," he says. "If you expect yourself to comprehend instantly the total meaning of the child's communication and to heal immediately the child's grief, chances are that you will do a poor job of listening. If you find yourself being impatient in your effort to understand, you may unknowingly be treating the aftermath of the death in the child's life as an event rather than a process."

Dr. Wolfelt explains that another sign that we may be trying to move our children through the grief experience too quickly is when we find ourselves talking *at* our children instead of listening to them. "Unfortunately, there are times when out of our sense of urgency to help the child we become more concerned with 'preaching' to the child than with listening and responding. Hopefully, we can recognize that we do not have to attempt to be all-wise and all-knowing to our children."

How much do children really understand?

For those who think babies, toddlers, and preschoolers are too young to understand that something terrible has happened, think again. Even the youngest children can sense when there is something wrong in their families, their households, and their normally secure environments. They may not have the specifics, but they surely will know that the people around them are upset and that something is threatening their routine.

Dr. Alan Greene, a California-based pediatrician who answers parents' questions on grief and other topics via his Web site, says that babies only hours old can pick up on a change in emotion in their parents. When mothers are grieving or depressed, children—from infants to teens—notice it and are affected by it. Their emotions, activities, and development can be shaped by the grief going on around and inside them.

"Kids are so wise about this stuff," he says. "They are extraordinarily emotionally perceptive, and when there is a loss in the family, even if it's somebody they don't know, they pick up on the grief of the others around them."

Dr. Greene explains that while kids are often more perceptive than adults in sensing what's happening emotionally, they are not good at articulating it or understanding it consciously. "It's something that impacts them," he says. "They react and respond to it, but they often are not able to say that they are grieving. That is true for infants who are not verbal but even for teens who are quite verbal but will often not make the connection between what's happening in their lives and the grief event that's going on. People want so much to shield kids from grief, but the truth is that once they have a loss they will grieve for at least a year. To leave them alone in their grief, to isolate them, obviously is the worst thing we can do for them."

As parents we often feel uncomfortable bringing up the subject of grief, or sharing our own pain with our children. We think that they are too young to experience such heartache. But children will experience grief with or without our help. It is up to us as parents to get involved and let them know that it's OK to be sad and to help them mourn in healthy ways. We just need to meet them where they are and to try to understand the world from their points of view.

According to Linda Goldman, a Maryland-based behavioral therapist who specializes in grief counseling, there are several developmental stages in which children have different views of death. One that she considers among the most crucial is what famed child psychologist Jean Piaget classified as the *preoperational stage,* which is marked by magical thinking, egocentricity, and reversibility.

Goldman says that at this stage a five-year-old may know that his grandfather is buried in the ground but will still write him a letter, put it in the mail, and expect to receive a letter from his grandfather in return. "Young kids also think that their wishes and thoughts make things happen," she explains. "It's really marked by the five-year-old who says, 'I hate you. I wish you were dead.' The next morning the brother is killed. The five-year-old thinks that his words magically created that, and the words may haunt him through adulthood."

As children move beyond magical thinking, they begin to enter what Piaget referred to as *concrete operation*. At this point, children have a more realistic idea of age span. They're curious and want to know the facts about things, including death. An explanation that may have satisfied a five-year-old is no longer acceptable, says Goldman, and they begin to put together bits and pieces of information until they fill in the whole story.

As children reach adolescence, any grief they experience as a result of a loss is compounded by the normal difficulties of being a teenager. They are already pulling away from their parents, seeking their independence, leaning more on their peers. When a death comes along, they often pull farther away, making it difficult or impossible to get them to open up to anyone but a close friend.

Goldman says that it helps for teens to have a peer support group. "Part of the teenage stage is self-absorption, being preoccupied with the present, and thinking that they're invulnerable. They tend to look toward their peers for support. That's a key piece."

How can we talk with our children about death?

It is never easy to talk about death. Turn on any animated movie with a heart-wrenching death scene, and most parents begin to squirm. How do we explain the death of Bambi's mother? Should we even sing the "Rock-a-Bye Baby" lullaby with its boughs breaking and cradles falling? And don't get us started on "Humpty Dumpty" or "The Three Little Pigs."

So many children's movies, fairy tales, and rhymes are filled with images of death, loss, and sadness. Most of us grew up on these favorites without a second thought to their deeper significance—that is until we had children of our own and really started listening to the words. Should we avoid all children's entertainment that includes death and sadness? No, says pediatrician Alan Greene and other experts on childhood development.

"There is children's literature that does have death and renewal in it," says Dr. Greene. "Something like *The Lion King,* which is often disturbing for kids when they first see it, is a good kind of disturbing. It helps them to deal with real events."

Noah and I had already talked about Simba's daddy in *The Lion King,* but it was another of his favorite videos that really brought the subject home. One afternoon we were

watching *The Land before Time,* which includes a heartbreaking scene of the young dinosaur Little Foot and his
dying mother. After she dies and he is left alone, Little Foot
meets up with an older dinosaur, who listens to his sad tale.
Little Foot blames himself, blames his mother, talks about
his anger and his sick stomach. The older dinosaur nods
knowingly and assures him that the stomachache will go
away but that the longing to see his mother again will stay
for a very long time. Little Foot finds a "tree star" (a leaf)
and keeps it with him as a reminder of his mother.

That afternoon, Noah and I talked about what happened
to Little Foot's mommy. It wasn't fun, it wasn't comfortable,
and it forced me to walk the fine line of giving him enough
information without scaring him. The discussion prompted a
conversation about my own "mommy," who he knows died
"a long time ago," and my friend Bertha, whom he got to know
before a heart attack took her far too young, and our dog
Chester, who died when Noah was only a year old. Noah wants
to know—and needs to know—the whats and whys of this
thing called death that seems to rear its head from time to
time. Not that I can always answer every question; many times
I stumble my way through. Sometimes I'm afraid I'm doing
more harm than good, but in the end I think Noah is better off
and better prepared for events that lie ahead.

Like the dead sparrow on the sidewalk, everyday events
that prompt our children to ask questions remind us of the
cycle of life that is threaded through our days, months, and
years. From the dead spider on the kitchen floor to the leaves

falling gently from the oak tree in the front yard, we are given ample opportunity to talk about birth, death, and rebirth.

Grief specialist Linda Goldman says that children need to make sense of death. "They need to define death. 'Mommy, will you die too?' 'Will I die?' 'Can thoughts and wishes make someone die?' You need to be very careful of common clichés that hurt understanding, like saying that Dad went away on a trip. 'Well, why didn't he say good-bye or take me with him?'"

Although young children are able to understand a lot of what we tell them, they are not always able to express back to us what they are feeling. We can talk to them about death in simple ways, maybe relating the loss of a friend or loved one to a similar event in one of their favorite books or perhaps to the death of an elderly neighbor, a pet, or even the pretty flowers they picked for Mom last Mother's Day.

Our motto should be Keep It Simple. Yes, sometimes people die. Their bodies don't work anymore, and so they can't go on living and breathing. But their souls—the part of them that made them who they were—live on in heaven. Life is never over.

That's a concept that many adults have difficulty accepting, but it is something that bears mentioning and repeating throughout a child's changing life.

How do we manage that first good-bye?

Some farewells will be easier for our children to take, and those are perfect opportunities to explore the subject and

find those "teachable moments" we so often hear about.
When the pet goldfish dies, it is not silly to hold a good-bye
ceremony, complete with eulogy and burial. (For more
specific information on ritual and memories, see chapter 9.)
It may seem excessive to us parents, but to a child it is often
a first glimpse of how we mark the passing of someone from
one life to the next. It gives the child a chance to see that
we honor the dead, celebrate their lives, and pray for them in
the next life. Granted it may be Goldie the Goldfish we're
praying for at the moment, but one day it will be someone
much dearer, and it will be easier because Goldie paved the
way. Even allowing a child to attend the funeral of a distant
relative can help prepare him for the day that he will be asked
to do the same for a grandparent, parent, or friend.

We took Noah with us to the wake of my brother-in-law's
grandmother. Noah had met "Gammaw" on several occasions,
and I had told him that she died. Even though he was only
three at the time, we opted to allow him to go up to the casket
with us and ask questions. He wasn't scared or crying or even
shy. He asked questions about her and about the box she was
in, and he will from time to time mention "Gammaw" when
we're talking about people or things that have died.

By letting children be aware of more distantly connected
people who are dying or have died, says Dr. Greene, we can
prepare them for the times when they are affected by deaths
that are close to them.

"I was recently working with a family who knew that the
grandmother was going to be dying very soon," he recalls.

"Rather than pretend that it wasn't happening, they put together a scrapbook of all the favorite memories they had of the grandmother. The kids drew pictures and made a whole good-bye gift for her. It was really hard, but it was really wonderful. And I'm sure they're going to do much better grieving than if they had not been prepared for it."

There is no way to avoid the hurt that comes with death, and so we have to learn to cope with it instead. We can become aware of our children's sensitivity to what is happening around them. People are crying; some may be angry. Dinner doesn't get made. The house is a mess. Mom doesn't ever seem to sleep. They will get caught up in all of it, and, if we don't talk to them, they will begin interpreting it for themselves—something that can be more frightening and more traumatic than hearing the truth. That's where we step in, take a deep breath, and begin the long grieving process by helping our children accept the reality and the finality of death.

WHAT SHOULD YOU SAY?

It is not a question of *if* your child will ask questions, but *when* they will ask questions. Below are some of the most common questions children may ask, depending on age, development, and how much they have been told. Don't use the following Q&A as a script but as a guide. Include only those topics that seem appropriate for your child and adapt them to fit your particular situation. Some questions listed in the preschool section may be asked by elementary-age children or even teens. That's OK. There are no hard-and-fast rules when it comes to grief and how children will respond. Just listen to their questions and answer them as honestly as you can.

TODDLER/PRESCHOOL Q&A

Q: What happens when you die?

A: Your heart stops beating. You stop breathing. Your skin loses its warmness. You don't feel anything anymore. You don't think. You don't hear or talk. You don't dream or wake up.

Q: Where do we go when we die?

A: We go to heaven to be with God. Even though our bodies don't work anymore, our souls—the part of us that makes us who we are—go to heaven and live forever. We believe that after we die we will be together in heaven with the people we love.

(continued)

Q: Are you going to die some day? Am I going to die?

A: Everybody has to die, but hopefully we will be around for a long, long time. Every person, every living thing, is born and lives and dies. It's part of life, and even though it's sad, God promises us that we can come and live with him when we're finished here on earth.

Q: Did Billy die because I was mean to him the other day?

A: No. We can't make people die by what we think or what we say. You didn't have anything to do with Billy's death— but it's normal to feel that way. We all feel bad when someone we love dies, and it's OK to cry or get angry. Just remember that people die because of sicknesses or accidents or old age. They don't die because of our thoughts, even when we have fights or get mad.

ELEMENTARY AGE Q&A

Q: What did Grandma die from?

A: Grandma died from cancer, which is a very bad disease. Her doctors gave her medicine to try to make it better, but Grandma was too sick. Her body was weak and couldn't keep working.

Q: I miss Spot. Why did he have to get hit by that car? I don't ever want to have another pet.

A: It's normal to feel that way. Spot was your buddy. He got out of the yard and ran into the street. That's why this happened. It was an accident. Nobody caused it.

I understand if you don't want to think about getting another pet. You can never replace Spot, and we wouldn't ever want to try. But maybe someday down the road you'll find a puppy that needs a home, just like when you found Spot.

Q: What's going to happen to us now that Dad is gone?

A: We are going to be together. I will always take care of you and love you and protect you. I know it's going to be hard without Dad, and we're all going to miss him terribly, but if we help each other, we can get through it. I am here to listen to you any time you want to talk or any time you just want a hug.

Q: Do I have to go back to school? I'm afraid the kids will make fun of me.

A: In a few days we'll go visit your teacher and the principal and talk about it. You do have to go back to school, and some kids might not know how to act, but it won't always be that way. As long as you let me know what's happening and what's on your mind, we can work through any problems together.

Q: Why did God take my sister away?

A: God didn't "take" her at all. She died in a car accident. God doesn't take people to reward or punish them or us. Sometimes bad things just happen, and we don't

(continued)

understand the reasons. We have to remember that God is here for us when we are scared or upset, even when we are mad at him. It's OK to feel angry at God. Sometimes I feel angry with God, too.

TEENAGE Q&A

Q: Why should I go to the wake and funeral? What difference is it going to make?

A: This is a time for us to get together with family and friends to remember Grandpa. It's a time to tell stories and share memories of someone we all loved. You don't have to go if you don't want to, but it is a really nice way to say one last good-bye. Think about it a little more before you make a decision. I'd love for you to come with us as long as you're comfortable.

Q: How can I believe in a loving God when he could let my friend get shot at school?

A: No one ever said believing would be easy, or that it would mean we would go through life without feeling any pain. God didn't shoot your friend. God didn't make this happen. A bad person made this happen, and it's OK to feel angry. It's normal to feel as if God let you down. Just try to lean on your friends and us while you're going through this. And remember, you can still pray and talk to God about what you're feeling.

Q: Why do I feel like such an outsider—even with my best friends?

A: When someone we love dies, it sets us apart from other people. Friends might not know what to say or do when they see us. For someone who's never lost a loved one, it's not always easy to understand just how bad it hurts. Try to be patient with them, but in the meantime maybe we could find a grief support group for kids your age. I think it would help to talk about this with people who have been through it. Maybe we could get you a journal so that you could express what you're feeling. Write, draw a picture, compose a song—whatever helps you get the feelings out. And always remember that you can come to me with anything that's on your mind.

TALKING ABOUT DEATH: A PRIMER

GETTING STARTED

- Be open and honest about how your loved one died.
- Acknowledge that you are sad and that it is OK for your child to feel sad.
- Ask your child how he feels and then sit back and listen.
- Give your child the opportunity to attend the memorial, wake, funeral, or burial services.
- Talk about the deceased loved one, remembering good times, looking through photos.
- Allow your child to use writing or drawing to let feelings out.

PITFALLS TO AVOID

- Don't assume your child is too young to understand what is happening.
- Don't tell your child stories that could be confusing. For instance, don't tell your child that Grandma went away on a long trip or that the recently deceased neighbor went to sleep and never woke up.
- Don't mask your own feelings or pretend that you are not affected by the death.
- Don't force your child to attend funeral services against her will, and don't refuse to let your child attend if she wants to be there.
- Don't make the deceased loved one a taboo subject.
- Don't ignore signs that your child is in pain or in need of professional help.

A Letter to a Loved One

Writing a letter to a loved one may help your child figure out what he is feeling and why. Your child doesn't have to be a budding poet or novelist to put pen to paper. Simply encourage him to follow the steps below.

STEP 1. Get a few sheets of stationery, a spiral-bound notebook, or a fancy journal—whichever best suits your needs and style.

STEP 2. Begin your letter as though you are simply writing a real letter to the person you love. If that is too difficult, write the letter to someone else who is close to you. Remember, no one else will see this, so feel free to express whatever comes to your mind. Try not to leave out the scary parts or things you think other people wouldn't like. Just let your feelings flow.

STEP 3. Talk about what you have been doing since you last saw your loved one. Have you been out much, keeping up with friends and hobbies, back to school or work? Do you have a hard time doing the things you used to do?

STEP 4. Talk about how you miss your loved one. Do you miss having someone to talk to, someone to kiss you goodnight, someone to walk with you to the bus stop, someone to eat lunch with at school? Just think about everything that has changed since your loved one died, and try to capture how that makes you feel.

ACTIVITY

STEP 5. Describe what's going on around your house. How is your family faring? Are people acting differently toward you? Are things very quiet? Very chaotic? Do they seem unchanged? How does all this make you feel?

STEP 6. Once the letter is complete, put it somewhere special and reread it on your loved one's birthday, at holidays, or on the anniversary of his or her death. It may help to see how you were feeling at the time and how you have progressed.

Other Letter-Writing Options

If the letter is written immediately after a loved one's death, your child may want to leave it in the casket as part of her farewell. That's what I did when my grandmother died. I have no recollection of what that letter said. I remember pouring my heart out on paper, crying as I reread it, and quietly tucking it inside the casket just before I said my last good-bye. No one else knew that I did it, but I knew that I had left something special with my grandmother.

OPTION 1. If your child seems to find the letter writing helpful, encourage her to keep an ongoing journal of how she is feeling. She can write in letter form or in whatever form feels most comfortable.

OPTION 2. If a child is very young, a parent or other adult can tell the child to dictate a letter. Be sure to read the letter back to the child to be sure you are capturing what he is saying. Give the letter to the child to store in a safe place or keep it until he is old enough to read it for himself.

OPTION 3. Use the letter as part of your memory book or keep it in your memory box. (See "Creating a Memory Book" and "Alternate Memory Makers" in chapter 4 for more details on how to create these.)

OPTION 4. Instead of a letter, have your child write a tribute to your loved one. Ask other family members to do the same. Have everyone read them aloud at a family gathering in your loved one's honor.

3

A Shoulder to Lean On: Supporting Our Children As They Deal with Their Emotions

- **What are normal reactions to death?**

- **What emotions often accompany grief?**

- **How do children of different ages respond?**

- **What attitude in the parent is most helpful to the child?**

Nothing can make up for the absence of someone we love. . . . We must simply hold out and see it through.

Dietrich Bonhoeffer

I was mad because my mom didn't let me see my Aunt Irene before she died. She said I was too young, as if I would only remember the way she was right before she died. I could understand that if I was younger, but I was almost thirteen. So I was mad because I never got to say good-bye. . . .

When Mom didn't let me see Aunt Irene, I thought maybe she didn't look like herself anymore. To me she always looked like Aunt Irene, even at the wake. But I was old enough to remember all the things we did together. I was always really close to her.

After she died, I cried myself to sleep every night for two months. Nobody ever knew. I wrote a lot. I wrote in journals, and I wrote poetry. I made my confirmation just a couple of weeks after she died. Picking her name for my confirmation name was like keeping her with me. I still go to the cemetery all the time and talk to her. Whenever I'm debating something or unsure about something, I go to the cemetery and ask myself, *What would Aunt Irene say?*

—Colleen Venne

~

Confusion, anger, sadness, guilt, and fear: they all come with the territory when someone we love dies. When children suffer such a loss, those feelings are compounded by the fact that children are often isolated from the adults around them. But this is not the time for them to be alone. This is the time for us parents and other adults to ask them about their feelings, to watch for both the verbal and nonverbal messages they are sending out, to walk beside them as they experience some of these emotions for the first time.

As they begin the second task of grieving, children need to feel the powerful emotions of grief with their whole beings, and they need to find ways to cope with the meaning of those feelings in their lives. They may be scared by their own anger. They may be overcome with fear. They may be pulled into a sadness so deep and so painful that it makes them withdraw from the world. We can help ease the pain by letting them know that it's OK to have those feelings and that we are willing to talk or to listen or simply to be a comforting presence.

What are normal reactions to death?

As our children go through the early stages of grief, there will be some pretty typical outward signs of the emotional battle that is raging within. It is completely normal for a child to experience any or all of the following symptoms:

- Sleep disturbances
- Changes in appetite
- Headaches
- Stomach pain
- Regressive behavior
- Increased fears
- Anger
- Guilt
- Acting out in school
- Disinterest in school, sports, music lessons, etc.
- Concern about his own health or that of his parents, siblings, etc.

When these behavior changes continue for an extended period of time or intensify to a point where a child is unable to function at home or in school, outside help may be needed. Any signs of serious depression, any suicidal comments, or any indications of alcohol and drug abuse or violence are red flags that indicate a need for immediate help.

Pediatrician Alan Greene says that aggression is a very common way for kids to grieve. They may begin bullying others or allowing themselves to be bullied. "Inability to pay attention, ADD/ADHD symptoms, school performance dropping off—all of that is common, depending on the age level of the kids. Temper tantrums are very common in children up to four or five years old as part of grieving."

We can share our concerns about our children's grief symptoms with their pediatrician. Since the pediatrician may already be aware of our children's temperament, existing health problems, and religious and cultural background, she may be in the perfect position to watch for warning signs that require outside help and to advise family members on how to cope.

It also helps to notify teachers, teachers' assistants, baby-sitters, or anyone who spends regular time with our grieving children so that they, too, can watch for warning signs and alert us to potential problems.

What emotions often accompany grief?

Whether children are toddlers or teens or anywhere in between, they will be hit full force during the grieving process by an array of emotions that may take parents—and children themselves—by surprise. Especially for very young children, these may be feelings that they have never experienced before. They look to us for confirmation that it's OK to let those feelings out. If we don't allow our children to express their feelings of grief, those pent-up emotions may block them— academically, socially, intellectually, and spiritually—and prevent them later on from experiencing life fully.

Donna Schuurman, executive director of the Dougy Center in Portland, Oregon, says that the children who end up at her center often demonstrate behaviors that other people don't understand. They act distracted, skip homework, get into fights, lie, sleep more than usual, and disobey the rules in general. A lot of parents don't know how to react when their children stop talking to them or start "acting out," a term that should be struck from the bereavement vocabulary, according to Schuurman, since such behavior is, in reality, a cry for help that could save a child.

"Children act out the pain that's inside of them, and that's a good thing," she explains. "If we don't attend to them, they're going to have to keep igniting and making their actions louder and louder so that people won't keep missing them. What frequently happens is that people just slough it off, telling themselves that the child is just trying to get attention. Yes, they are trying to get attention, and if they don't get it, they're just going to have to keep doing more and more radical things."

The kids who seek support at the Dougy Center are all over the map—from setting fires to becoming completely truant. Schuurman recalls one girl who had been a straight-A student and a high-school cheerleader—until her boyfriend shot and killed himself in front of her because she was going to break up with him. In her shock, she ran—still covered in blood—to the local mall in search of a friend. Around school, however, the story deteriorated quickly, and she was cast as a selfish person who decided to go shopping after witnessing her boyfriend's suicide. It didn't take long before she stopped going to school and even stopped going home.

"Every other Thursday this girl would show up at the Dougy Center. Nobody was making her come here. She would just come and sit in the opening circle, and very often she would fall asleep. That was how she worked on her grief. Our center was a safe place to come and sleep," says Schuurman. "She's now in college. I shudder to think what would have happened if we had said, 'You can't come here and sleep.' So our process is very much geared toward trusting that by providing a safe place and acceptance, children and adults will do the grief work that they need to do."

Anger. Name an emotion that first comes to mind when you talk about a loved one's death, and anger will be at the top of the list. Children may be overcome by anger—with themselves, with their parents, with God—and that can affect their lives in powerful ways. We parents can watch for signs of that anger, such as a sudden urge to hit or throw things, a particular tone of voice, or even a new silence that hadn't been there before.

Gregory Floyd's young sons David and John Paul were hit by a car while playing outside their home in New Jersey. David survived; John Paul did not. David went to his father one day and said that he was a "teeny bit angry" with the man who hit them. Gregory used that moment of honesty to begin a conversation about feelings of anger and the idea of forgiveness.

"You don't want to talk about it prematurely. You want to validate their feelings. You want to say, 'Hey, this is very real for you to feel angry, and I'm not surprised. I'm not alarmed. I understand. I'm angry too, and it's a perfectly appropriate response to having life snatched away from you, but you don't want to stay there.' I told him that anger can be a cage that we get imprisoned in. Then we talked about forgiveness."

Lorraine Wilson, whose fourteen-year-old son Robby drowned on a Boy Scout outing, recalls how her young children reacted to their brother's death. "When the kids were younger, the biggest personality change I saw was in Peter (who was six when Robby died). He had always been such a gentle, happy little boy. He became very angry. He would hit me and tell me he hated me."

Anger is often a child's way of dealing with frustration, sorrow, pain, and confusion. It may not be easy to handle or pleasant to watch, but it is necessary for healing. We've all been on the receiving end of our children's anger at one time or another, even after minor incidents. Reach back and remember how you dealt with that anger in a positive way, then use that knowledge to deal with the anger now. The one thing we don't want to do is to make our children think that their anger is bad. Hidden anger now will turn into serious problems later.

Fear and separation anxiety. When Kathy Duke's four-year-old daughter, Emma, died of cancer, one of Kathy's first concerns was her son Joseph, who was just shy of his sixth birthday. Although Joe had been included in Emma's sickness and treatment from the very beginning, learning to cope without his sibling was another story. The Dukes called on a local hospice organization and joined a grief support group.

"The first three or four meetings, the counselor said that whenever they started talking about their feelings Joe would get up and walk away," says Kathy. "Finally one time he was there with just the counselor. He was asked to help set up. After that time, he felt like he was an integral part of the thing. He really opened up."

Joe was reacting in ways that are typical of children who lose a loved one. "He started having nightmares," Kathy explains. "The counselors told us that this was actually a positive and healthy thing because it meant that he was dealing with it on a certain level."

Kathy says that one of the most difficult parts of her son's grief was that he became so fearful. "He was devastated when Emma died. He had become quite independent, but after she died he wanted to stay right by us. He didn't want to go into another room without us. If my husband was five minutes late coming home, Joseph would just cry and cry and say, 'Daddy's been killed in a wreck.' If I had any piece of advice for other parents it would be to include the children as much as you possibly can. Be open to their feelings and what they're saying."

Guilt. One of the most common reactions kids have to death is guilt. Even if the death is the result of something they couldn't have had any control over, they often feel responsible when someone close to them dies.

Colleen Venne, who talked earlier in this chapter about her anger after missing the chance to say good-bye to her dying aunt, experienced her own misplaced guilt after her grandmother was hit by a car years earlier.

"I was nine when Nani died," recalls Colleen, now twenty-six. "I blamed myself. Until recently I thought that she had been coming to our house to watch me the day she was hit. I never knew that she wasn't, so up until two years ago I thought it was my fault. I blamed myself the whole time."

Such a reaction is extremely common, even though Colleen's mother, Margaret Robertson, says that she has no recollection of any comments or events that might have caused her daughter to feel that way. Children can create guilt where none exists. It's just another way that they deal with the difficult circumstances of grieving.

Relief. Although it may be shocking to hear, there will be times when our children feel relieved over the loss of a loved one. Some circumstances surrounding this reaction are pretty obvious: long illness, pain, suffering, a loved one who no longer looks or acts like he used to. For many children, death is a relief. That's not an easy thing to admit, so it's an especially troubling emotion for kids to negotiate and usually goes hand in hand with guilt.

There may be other more problematic reasons for children's feelings of relief. Some children may have been abused; some may have seen their loved one hurt himself or others. Whatever the reason, we can help our children work through this complicated grief by dropping our judgmental attitudes and letting them know that the feelings they are experiencing do not make them bad people.

How do children of different ages respond?

How can we explain death to children who can't yet express themselves? How can we help them accept a tragedy that is almost entirely beyond their comprehension? We have to rely on our own sense of what our children need and on our parental instinct, that same innate sense that makes us know without seeing that our children are sneaking a cookie before dinner or taking the car to a friend's house instead of the library. Children of every age will react to death in unique ways. We can be prepared, even if we can't anticipate every question or problem.

Babies. Babies will pick up on the tension in their environments and may even sense the stress in the arms of the people who are holding them. They will react to a parent's tears or anger. Although they do not yet walk or talk, they *do* feel.

A baby may simply need to be kept in some semblance of a normal routine—naps at nap time, dinner at 6 P.M., bedtime lullaby and good-night. But keeping a normal routine may not be so easy for a parent who is grieving. You may need to enlist the help of a relative or a friend who is close to your child.

Ask a friend to come over and play with your toddler every afternoon before nap time. See if a nearby relative is willing to visit every morning to get breakfast on the table and get the little ones dressed. It may sound like a lot to ask, but most friends are happy to help in a time of need, and, remember, it won't last forever.

Preschoolers. Young children experiencing grief may become more clingy or may suddenly be afraid of the dark. They may begin wetting the bed, eating differently, or wanting to sleep with parents. Such changes in behavior may be due, in large part, to their fear of what they don't understand. Our job, then, is to pay attention, offer a lot of reassurance, and keep the lines of communication open. We can begin by explaining some of the things that are probably most confusing to a three- or four-year-old.

Peggy Bohme, executive director of the Warm Place, a grief support center in Fort Worth, Texas, says that parents should deal with preschoolers by first giving them the very basics about what it means to be dead: You don't move; you don't breathe; you don't feel or hear anything; you don't eat or go to the bathroom. She lets the children use a stethoscope to listen first to a sidewalk and then to somebody's heart.

"Just telling them what is alive and what is dead is a big part of what needs to be done," says Bohme. "And feelings are important. What is a happy feeling and what is a sad feeling? We help them put words to those feelings."

My son, Noah, demonstrated a classic example of how preschoolers use simple emotional terms to understand complex concepts. When he was three, he asked about the photograph of my mother that sat on the bookcase in our living room. I explained that he didn't know this grandma because she died a long time ago. He put down his snack and with a look of confusion on his face said, "But she looks happy in the picture." She was smiling, so how could she be dead, which in his mind equaled sad?

That's how preschoolers operate. They call on simple emotions they understand—happy, sad, mad, scared—to explain more difficult subjects. But simplifying things doesn't necessarily clear up their confusion.

Gregory Floyd's daughter Rose, who was four when her brother John Paul died, came down to breakfast the day after his funeral and asked, "Where's Johnny?"

"That just threw us across the room mentally. You wonder, 'How could she not get this?' We weren't mad at her, but it was simply amazing," Gregory says. "She watched his coffin go into the ground yesterday, and she's wondering where he is. I think that is the mercy of God because I think the Lord draws a veil and unveils that veil a bit at a time according to what the children are intellectually and emotionally capable of dealing with."

Elementary-school kids. As children move out of the preschool stage and into the elementary-school age, their feelings of grief begin to change, with heavy emphasis on magical thinking during the early elementary years. If a child wished a person were dead at some point, he thinks the death was his fault. And even if he understands on some level that dead means gone forever, he expects the person to return.

Think fairy tales and cartoons, and you'll have some idea of what's going through your child's mind. Snow White and Sleeping Beauty come back from what appear to be deathlike states. Road Runner and Wile E. Coyote, Tom and Jerry, Elmer Fudd and Daffy Duck—none of them ever succumbs to the things that would kill a real person. Kids at this stage are on that wavelength. Death is reversible to them. It's forever, but what does forever mean to an eight-year-old?

Young children often cannot sit down and explain to us how they feel, but there are other ways to help them to express their fears, confusion, and anger. We can give them crayons and ask them to draw, or take them outside and let them run off the steam that is building up inside of them. Grief is not the time to ask our children to sit quietly and avoid play and laughter. In fact, it is often through playing and acting "normal" that they are able to protect themselves from the shock of death and begin to process the information in ways they can handle. Let them kick a ball around the yard or pound a piece of clay. Think of how nice it would be if we could do the same when the pressure of grief gets to be too much for us.

Lorraine Wilson took her three children with her to meetings of the Compassionate Friends, a grief support organization. There the children would draw pictures that gave her insights into what they were thinking. "The kids knew Robby wanted to fly, so one of them drew a picture of him in an airplane. He said, 'Here I am flying in Robby's airplane. I don't want to come down.' That's how they would express their feelings."

Older children may prefer to write down their feelings in a journal or ask questions of their parents, clergy, or other close adults. They may want to help plan the funeral or participate in the funeral Mass or memorial service. But first they need to be invited. Elementary-age children as well as pre-adolescents need to know that we welcome their questions and their presence.

Teenagers. Teenagers may react to grief by not seeming to react at all. They may appear disinterested, as if the death has not affected their day-to-day lives. Over time, however, that reaction begins to wear thin and other signs of unprocessed grief begin to surface.

Although teens may experience many of the same physical symptoms as younger children in grief, their reactions may surface in stronger, more dangerous doses. What may be a temporary decrease in appetite for a preschooler can become a full-blown eating disorder for a teen. An increased tendency to pick school-yard fights for an eight-year-old can turn into a violent streak in a teen that makes him a danger to himself or others. Of course those are the extremes, but any of the following symptoms can be early warning signs that outside help is necessary:
- Stomach problems, changes in appetite, eating disorders
- Headaches, sleep disturbances

- Aggression, anger, violent tendencies
- Demonstrating new or worrisome behavior around the home, neighborhood, or school
- Falling grades, truancy
- Isolation, withdrawal, depression
- Rebellion against parents, authority figures, religion
- Personality changes—from introvert to extrovert or vice versa
- Change of friends
- Alcohol and drug use
- Sexual promiscuity
- Statements or actions that hint at suicidal thoughts

While some of these symptoms can be found in any teen going through a difficult adolescence, all of them can be directly related to grief. The last three—alcohol and drug use, sexual promiscuity, and suicidal tendencies—should prompt immediate action and a call to a healthcare professional who is trained to deal with such behavior. Do not wait, thinking that it's just a typical teenage phase. Act swiftly, and you may be able to avoid devastating consequences.

The majority of teens will go through some form of the less severe symptoms without getting pulled down into dangerous terrain. The key, experts say, is for us parents to pay attention to what our children are doing or saying. Any sudden or profound transformation in behavior, attitude, or physical appearance is a sign that a child is struggling with something deeper.

Teens may have many questions but won't necessarily want to ask their parents or other authority figures. Often they will pull away from their families and rely on the support of their peers. A lack of emotion and a reliance on friends are typical of teens caught in the tug-of-war between childhood and adulthood.

We must make ourselves available to them. Don't judge or yell, push or ignore. The issue calls for a delicate balance, but so do most issues when it comes to parents and teens. We can't be afraid to look for outside support, even if it's "only" another empathetic teen who is willing to listen to whatever our children have to say.

What attitude in the parent is most helpful to the child?

Probably one of the hardest realities for us parents to deal with is the fact that we cannot take away our children's grief. We feel helpless knowing that our children are hurting, aching, longing for someone, and that we cannot fill the void. When we are grieving ourselves, the process is even more painful. We don't have the energy; we don't have the objective perspective; we don't have the physical or emotional ability to pull ourselves out of our own pain to see our children's grief in a clear and distinct way.

Remember Colleen Venne from the beginning of this chapter? Her missed opportunity to say one last good-bye before her aunt's death has stayed with her into adulthood, but it had its beginnings in her own mother's grief.

Her mother, Margaret Robertson, can remember with vivid detail the night Colleen wanted to see her dying aunt. Margaret's sister, Irene, was lying in a bed in her family room fighting to stay alive. Her cancer had progressed so far in those final days that she was unable to walk or eat or even hold a conversation. Margaret says that the main reason she did not bring her daughter for a visit was because she did not believe her sister was that close to death. She was hoping for a miracle, she says, or at least for a few more days. She never imagined that death would come so quickly.

So without a doubt, our own grief affects our children's grief. As parents we can share our feelings with our children and let them know that we're hurting too. That's a good beginning. Although our children like to believe that we have all the answers, sometimes it's good for them to see us struggling alongside them.

Despite our best efforts to talk and listen, however, sometimes our children are going to need more help than we can give them. If they demonstrate behaviors that cause us concern, there is a multitude of ways to help: counselors who specialize in grief or child development, grief support programs specifically for children, art therapy programs, church-sponsored bereavement programs, clergy counseling, close relatives and friends (see referrals in "Resources for Healing").

When we start worrying that our children are not reacting appropriately, we can stop and think back to little Joseph Duke whose nightmares were actually positive signs and whose initial fears and anxieties were part of healthy grieving. Children react differently to death than adults do. Although they may want to play baseball in the middle of a memorial service, they are hurting on the inside. Play and laughter are ways they can escape the grief, if only for a moment, and gather their strength for the rest of the process.

Peggy Bohme compares children in grief to a ball being pushed under water: no matter how hard you push it down,

DANGER SIGNS

All children may show milder forms of the behaviors listed below. However, when a behavior progresses to dangerous levels that can cause your child or others harm in any way, it is time to seek immediate professional help. If you have any doubts about whether your child's behavior warrants outside help, go ahead and seek it. Counselors, grief support groups, pediatricians, clergy members, and other professionals will be able to assist you in your quest to help your child heal. It is better to seek outside help too soon than to wait until it is too late. Below are the most common danger signals:

- Aggression—picking fights, hitting or kicking, setting fires, throwing things, talking in violent terms it pops back up again. "Children will grieve intently and then come up for air," she says. "They can only absorb so much and then they need to play baseball or go to a movie or sit and do their homework."

We can let our children know that they are not bad or strange because of how they feel and that it's OK to play and laugh and work and cry. As parents we can sit back and let our children show us what they need—whether it's a trip to the ice-cream parlor or a heart-to-heart talk at the kitchen table.

- Complete withdrawal from family life—isolation, disinterest in life in general, complete silence, eating or sleeping disturbances that have the potential to create health problems
- Refusal to go to school, refusal to participate in usual activities
- Fears that interfere with normal activities, such as sleep, meals, school, play
- Regressive behaviors that go on for an extended period— thumb sucking, bed-wetting, sleeping with parents, baby talk
- Lying to parents, teachers, friends
- Depression

(continued)

- Indifference or denial that never progresses to expressions of grief
- Alcohol or drug use or sexual promiscuity in older children
- Suicidal thoughts or actions—talking about suicide, giving away personal belongings, any sign that a child is desperately seeking attention or help

WORKING THROUGH ANGER

Every child gets angry. Sometimes it's over something no more serious than a broken toy; other times it is over the devastation of a broken heart. Use your knowledge of your own child to guide you through this normal part of the grief cycle. Here are some additional tips for helping your child work through anger:

- Acknowledge the anger and don't give in to the urge to squelch it. Your child needs to express these feelings or they will build up under the surface.
- Let your child know it's normal to feel angry under the circumstances.
- Share your own experiences with similar anger. Maybe you were mad at some time because someone you loved died (or moved away, or became ill). Let your child know that you understand these feelings.
- Try to help your child move past the anger. Ask what is making her mad—that Mom didn't fight harder to get well, that Dad won't be here to coach Little League anymore, that Grandma won't be around to read stories and go for walks, that Spot won't be here to sleep on the end of the bed.
- If your child is expressing anger toward God, let him know that it's OK. Then try to talk about God, how God doesn't "take" people away from us, how we can turn to God even in our anger.

ACTIVITY

Anger Buster

Use the following activity to help your child get her feelings of anger out in the open. Don't be afraid to alter the activity to better suit your child.

STEP 1. Take a moment to talk about your deceased loved one with your child.

STEP 2. Give your child a lump of modeling clay or Play-Doh and table space to work.

STEP 3. Turn on some dramatic music (classical or whatever best suits you and your child).

STEP 4. Let your child pound the clay to the beat of the music.

STEP 5. Allow your child to pound, stretch, roll, and tear the clay in order to let out pent-up feelings in an acceptable way. (This may also give you some insight into the way your child is really feeling.)

STEP 6. Experiment with different kinds of music in different environments.

STEP 7. Feel free to grab a piece of clay and join in. You may be surprised at how much it helps.

Don't limit this exercise to a one-time event. Use it whenever there's a lot of tension in the air. Remember that this activity is not supposed to be a chore. It should be healing, expressive, and most of all fun.

Alternate Anger-Busting Activities

You don't have to limit yourself and your child to clay pounding. Expand this music-based activity to include other mediums, such as painting or dancing.

OPTION 1. Give your child paint and allow him to use brushstrokes and color choices to reflect his feelings.

OPTION 2. Tell your child to dance or move to the music. Provide plenty of open space and maybe some scarves or rhythm sticks and maracas to add to the fun.

OPTION 3. Let your child take a turn at choosing the music and medium.

ACTIVITY

4

Gone Forever: Helping Children Adjust to Permanent Loss

- How can we help our children adjust?

- Where do we begin?

- What are some issues that hamper adjustment?

- How long will it take?

The experience of loss does not wait for children to grow into adulthood.
Alan Wolfelt, *Helping Children Cope with Grief*

My brother, Fred, was eighteen when our mother began the final days of her fight with colon cancer. As she slipped into a coma, Fred acted as though nothing in his life was changing. He stayed in his room with the television on, while the rest of us kept vigil around our mother's bed. He went out with his girlfriend on dates, while we cried over what we knew was surely the end.

On our mother's final night, Fred was up in his room as usual. Although the rest of us were keenly aware of the fact that my mother might not live until morning, Fred had yet to visit her bedside in the family room for one last good-bye. Finally, I went up to his bedroom, knocked on the door, and told him point blank what he had been trying to avoid: Our mother was dying, and if he did not say good-bye now, he would never again have the chance.

Fred came into the family room, walked over to a corner, slumped down onto the ground, and began to cry. He slept with the rest of the family on the floor that night, and he was there when our mother came out of her coma at 5 A.M. that April morning for one last glimpse of her family and her final battle for breath.

The months that followed were particularly hard on Fred, who was due to graduate from high school in June. Suddenly baseball games, proms, and parties weren't important. He gave up playing baseball. He went through the motions of graduation with our father alongside him and me in our mother's place at the ceremony.

Not long after, I moved across the country, causing Fred to suffer a second—although much less significant—loss. A year later our father remarried, and soon after that our sister, Tricia, followed me to Texas. For Fred it was like experiencing abandonment and loss over and over again. It made it hard for him to adjust to his initial and overwhelming grief over our mother's death. It would have been hard for anyone to adjust to that much change in such a short time, but being a teenager on the verge of adulthood made it that much harder.

✍

Fred's behavior during our mother's death and his subsequent difficulty with the grief that followed provide a textbook example of what teenagers do when they are confronted with the death of a close relative or friend. They withdraw, pretend they are not affected, and act as though death cannot touch them, even when it is just down the hall.

Those feelings of immortality and that attitude of disinterest can carry them through the early days or months of grief—but eventually, everything catches up with them. They soon realize that even they must stop to grieve and find a way to learn to live within a new kind of framework.

That is what this third task of grieving is about: helping our kids learn to live without their deceased loved one. We can foster this through rituals and commemorations that keep the person's memory alive. We can light a candle or write a poem. We can share stories about our loved ones. We can avoid compounding our children's grief by throwing additional stresses at them. This phase of grief is not about learning to forget but about learning to remember in a balanced, healthy way.

My best friend, Robin Gerrow, remembers how her ten-year-old son, Nathan Rhodes, reacted to their elderly dog's death. "We really didn't have any kind of ceremony when Grendel died. Nathan took it a lot harder than I expected. I didn't think he even liked the dog very much. He knew Grendel was sick but was still surprised at his death. The day he died, we made a point of having dinner together—a rare occasion—and telling our favorite stories about him. We laughed a lot and cried even more, but I think it was helpful that Nathan saw that we could do both at the same time. We could remember the good times and the times that Grendel was a real pain, and still love and miss him."

That's a key piece of information for us parents: We can show our children how to grieve by opening ourselves up to them. We cannot expect them to sit down and pour out their hearts if ours are locked against them. They need to see that we are human, too: that we cry and laugh, that we get angry and sad. They need to know that we will not cast a disapproving eye if they need to express their grief in front of us.

How can we help our children adjust?

Our children, regardless of age or developmental stage, need to learn how to adjust to the new circumstances of their lives if they are going to work through their grief and emerge healthy and whole. Sometimes that will be a monumental task, like adjusting to life without a mother or father. Other times it will be difficult but manageable, such as when a distant relative or a favorite pet dies.

We can help our children understand that even though life can never be exactly the same, it will go on. We can let them know that we don't expect them to pick up where they left off before the death. And we can hold out the possibility that at some point their day-to-day life will begin to feel "normal" again. To do that, however, we have to be willing to show our kids by example what they have to do.

If we have locked ourselves away, or given up friends and favorite hobbies, how can our children ever think it is OK to move on with their own lives? As parents we can send a powerful message that life goes on, that the person we lost wouldn't want us to sit alone crying every day.

Peggy Bohme says that learning to adjust is especially difficult because our society does not respect people in grief. "Death is really considered defeat in our society. People who have not gone through this do not have any idea what is needed until it comes to their own door. It's so overwhelming. Your family is gone; it's a new family. It's a one-parent family, or a one-child family, or a childless family. All of that changes dramatically overnight, and you're expected to forget it."

I can remember cleaning out my mother's dresser after her death and not being able to part with a certain sweater or a favorite dress. Slowly, over the months that followed, I learned to give up those things. Now I have a few select items that remind me of my mother: a birthday letter she left on my pillow years before she became ill, her treasured mother ring, a black cashmere sweater she gave me one Christmas. Although the sweater is getting ratty and the letter is tattered, these things have a physical connection to my mother, and for that reason they are special to me.

It's impossible—and unhealthy—to forget a deceased loved one or friend. In addition to the physical reminders, like the empty chair at the dinner table or the roadside cross marking where a friend died in a car wreck, people are likely to say things to us and to our children that will make us cringe, or cry. ("At least you still have a son," someone told a woman I spoke with who recently lost a daughter to cancer.) Others will tell us how to deal with our grieving children in less-than-helpful ways. ("Just buy him an identical puppy. He'll never know the difference.") Amid all this, we expect our children—and ourselves—to adjust. That's a tall order, but it's not out of our reach.

In her book *How to Go On Living When Someone You Love Dies,* grief expert Therese Rando says that after a person dies it takes a while for us to understand completely all of the roles he played in our lives. Learning to "be in the world" without our loved one reshapes the way we live.

"Readjustment to the new world without your loved one takes great patience and much practice," she says. "It is achieved painfully, step-by-step, as you gradually come to grips with that person not being in your life as he was before." We can remember those words as we work through the grieving process and wait expectantly for our children to do the same. They, too, will be struggling to fill the holes left by their loved one's absence while at the same time keeping that loved one's memory alive in their hearts.

Where do we begin?

Talking about our deceased loved one is a good place to start the adjustment process. It may bring back sad memories, but it's a necessary step for everyone's sake. Next we can create ways to commemorate the lives of our deceased loved ones, whether through formal events or homemade memorials.

- Look through photo albums and ask your children to share memories of your loved one.

- Visit your loved one's favorite restaurant, park, or museum on a birthday or anniversary.
- Plant a tree or flower in memory of your loved one and have your children create a special marker.
- Ask your children to make a Christmas ornament that will hang on the tree each year in your loved one's memory.
- Visit the cemetery on special occasions, and allow your children to decide what flowers or other mementos to bring.
- Ask your children to go through their toys and choose some to donate to a charitable organization in your loved one's name.
- Encourage your children to draw pictures or write stories about the times they shared with your loved one. Allow them to share or talk about their creations.
- When the time comes, include your children in the process of cleaning out your loved one's house or giving away your loved one's mementos when appropriate.
- Encourage your children to volunteer with or donate a small gift to your loved one's favorite charity.
- Let your children light a candle the next time they're in church, or allow them to light one at home and say a special prayer.
- Create a memory book filled with photos and stories of your loved one.

On his pediatrics Web site, Dr. Alan Greene recommends that a parent help her three-year-old son create a scrapbook of memories about his deceased grandfather. "Include lots of photos and memorabilia, but focus on getting your child's memories into tangible form," he says. "Ask him to draw pictures of the things he remembers about his grandfather, then ask him to tell you about the picture. Write down whatever your child says, and when he is finished, read it back to him. Give him the opportunity to add or change what he says until it clearly expresses what he is feeling. In this way you will not only help your child capture memories of his grandfather that will be with him for the rest of his life, but you will help your son clarify his current feelings."

Dr. Greene also suggests creating a video in which family members and close friends recount memories of their deceased loved one. Children can be involved in the process by sharing thoughts, asking questions, or just watching and listening. No one needs to be pressured to participate, but offering the opportunity is a way to let family members deal with their feelings and create a lasting memorial at the same time.

A remembrance can be anything we want it to be, but it should always include our children. They may even come up with memorial ideas of their own. We should allow them to explore and express their feelings, always remembering that no loss is too small or insignificant to commemorate.

When our German shepherd, Chester, died three years ago, we took his leather collar—complete with identification and rabies tags—and buckled it to the handle of my son's wagon. A little piece of Chester is always with us when we visit the park. We also bought a small, bone-shaped dog tag and had Chester's name, birth year, and death year etched into it. We tied a red ribbon through it, and each year we hang it on the Christmas tree. Finally, we buried Chester's ashes, along with his first rabies tag and a few dog biscuits, under the big oak tree in our front yard and put a statue of St. Francis of Assisi on top as a marker. Noah knows that Chester is buried there, and he considers it a favorite play spot for piling rocks and raking dirt. It's our way of letting him know that even though we now have another dog, we will never forget the one who came before. And it shows him that every life—even a dog's—is worth remembering and celebrating.

What are some issues that hamper adjustment?

No matter how hard we try to avoid them, inevitable road-blocks will get in the way of our children's adjustment to their new lives. We can't remove the people who will make insensitive comments. We can't fill the void left by a loved one's physical absence. We can't make our children move through grief more quickly in order to get to a healthy, adjusted place. What we can do is be especially aware of circumstances that may add to their grief.

Financial worries. Often a death in the immediate family can spell financial disaster for the survivors. Funeral costs, loss of salary, insurance issues, mortgages, and other expenses may suddenly become a burden. If a father dies in a car crash, for example, questions about finances that were never really a concern before may now become evident to children. Their mother may need to go out to work for the first time, or take on a second job. They may have to move to a smaller house. They may have to go to day care for the first time. For a child who is trying to accept the loss of a parent, confronting those additional worries makes this adjustment period more difficult.

Although it's not easy, we should try to keep financial issues close to the vest. Our children will overhear or pick up on some things, but the major worries should not be piled on their shoulders. When it gets to be too much for us to bear alone, we can call on sympathetic friends, counselors, or support groups.

Donna Schuurman of the Dougy Center says that responses to such circumstances will vary depending on an individual family's financial situation and the ways people deal with stress. Some families may, in fact, be better off financially after the death of a parent and spouse because of life insurance. Others may be pushed to the brink of bankruptcy or worse. Although our children cannot help but be caught up in some of the stress that money can cause, they cannot be so involved that their grief is overshadowed by their worry.

"It's a tricky role, not to overburden children and not to make them into premature adults, but also not to withhold information that they can sense," says Schuurman. "You don't want to think of everything in catastrophic terms, but on the other hand, for some people some things are going to have to change. Kids feel like their childhood is being taken away from them."

Role confusion. When a child loses a sibling or a parent, the family order is disrupted. Perhaps the oldest child is gone, throwing a younger child into the position of eldest for the first time. Or, in an even more dramatic family shift, a surviving sibling is now an only child. Or, a parent dies, and a child is expected to fill the void in either practical or emotional ways.

Without our even realizing it, we parents and other adults can add to our children's trauma by expecting them to take on new roles that may not be appropriate. It's not uncommon for a child to hear that she will have to "take care of the family" now that her mother is gone. Boys will inevitably hear that they must be the "man of the house" when their father dies. No child should be expected to take on such an enormous role, especially that of a parent. Attempting to do so while struggling to adjust to life without a loved one will only make this grief task more difficult.

Sonora Thomas, whose sister Eliza was brutally murdered in Austin, Texas, in 1991, says that her own grief was hampered by the fact that she spent most of her time worrying about her grieving parents instead of trying to heal herself.

"I always tried to make my parents happy," she says. "For a long time I felt more sorry for them than I did for myself. I tried everything I could to make the painful feelings go away." When she finally realized that she wasn't responsible for her parents' happiness or grief, she was able to move on to her own grief needs.

New stresses. Keep in mind that this is not the time to institute any other dramatic changes in a child's life—if there is any way we can avoid it. Moving to a new home or town immediately after the death of a parent, for instance, could prove to be beyond traumatic. Suddenly the child is ripped away from the places that hold all the memories of the deceased loved one. The routines, the sights and sounds of life before Dad died are not only all wrong because he is missing but also because the child has been removed from the scene of the relationship.

Changing schools, talking about divorce, even a parent taking on a new job can compound the effects of grief on a child. This is a time when security and stability are needed more than ever.

Donna Schuurman says that routine provides kids with a sense of comfort. "If a child has to move, he loses his school, his current friends, his home. It has a multiple impact. We encourage people to establish consistency and routines, because even things like dinnertime are usually completely changed if there is a death in the immediate family."

Creating taboos and fueling fantasies. We may find
ourselves creating stories that we think will help our children
deal with their loss. We pretend Grandpa went on a long trip.
We say that our dog was sent to live at a farm with lots of
room to roam. We stop talking about our deceased spouse or,
even worse, forbid our children from talking about their
deceased loved one.

It may start out as a well-meaning attempt to protect our
kids from too much pain too soon, but before long these
actions backfire and we find ourselves with bigger problems.
Miriam Klotz, a social worker with Hospice Austin in Texas, says
that one of the keys to helping our children come to terms with
a loved one's absence is to make sure that we don't turn the
person's name, memory, and favorite foods and activities into
taboo subjects. This behavior creates an unhealthy atmosphere
that encourages our children to live in a private fantasy world
"This is crucial," says Klotz, "because otherwise what you're
saying is that this part of your life is no longer allowed."

It comes back to the truth. If we withhold it, our kids
will create stories to fill in the blanks. We're better off taking a
deep breath, sitting down with our children, and saying all the
things that we don't want them to hear from someone else.

How long will it take?

Adjusting to life without a loved one is something that our
children should be allowed to do at their own pace. It may
take months before a child is ready to return to the athletic

field knowing that her dad will not be there to cheer for her. Maybe she will never play a particular sport again. That's OK, as long as she knows that it's not a betrayal of her father to go out and kick the soccer ball.

Carol Hyrcza, whose three-year-old son, Peter, drowned during a family outing, remembers how difficult it was for her son Andrew to adjust to life without his brother and best friend. Peter and Andrew had been inseparable, but on the day of the accident, Andrew went out in a boat with the older children while Peter stayed on the shore with his father. It's not all that surprising, then, that Andrew felt guilty because he did not stay with his brother. As his grief progressed, he had a hard time getting past that guilt.

"When there were other kids around, and he should have been having a fun time, Andrew would get really quiet. I would tell him, 'I know you're thinking of Peter, and he's here now. He'll always be with you.' We talked a lot. Every day we talked about Peter's death. Andrew would say, 'I wonder what he is doing now?' I had him draw pictures. We would go to the cemetery. I would write in a journal, and he would draw pictures of him and Rock (Peter) playing. I would write what they were doing because there was always a story behind the pictures. Now that he is older, he still writes in a journal because he doesn't want to forget any more than I do about those times that we had with Peter."

There really isn't any way that our children can forget such losses, nor would we want them to. Remembering our deceased loved ones brings them closer for a moment. We hear a favorite song, and for a few brief minutes we imagine that person singing and smiling. We smell apple pie baking in the oven and are taken back to days we will always cherish. Our children need to have those memories as well, but they need to learn that they cannot live in their memories forever.

We can watch for behaviors that might signal a need for intervention—if our preschooler is talking to his deceased father every day as if he is still alive, if our elementary-age child continues filling the dog's food dish every day months after he's gone, if our preadolescent starts taking on personality traits of her deceased sibling, if our teen becomes obsessed with death and violence.

Balance is a key word here. All of the behaviors mentioned above may happen at one time or another as part of the normal grieving process, but when they begin to take on increasing significance in our children's lives or start to alter their ability to cope with reality, help is needed. If we know how to read our children, we can intervene before behavior gets out of hand.

Think about how long it takes us adults to adjust to new situations. How many months must pass before we feel comfortable in a new job? How long before we finally get around to calling a new city "home"? How much harder is it, then, for a child to get used to going to bed every night without a kiss and a prayer from Mom? It takes time—and in some ways, it takes forever. It takes a willingness to travel through sadness to a place of acceptance. And, as you will read in the next chapter, it takes a mountain of trust for a child to open his heart and begin to love and live again.

ACTIVITY

CREATING A KID-FRIENDLY MEMORIAL FOR A PET

Your child will probably surprise you with his ability to create a memorial without any input from you. But if your child is looking for some ideas on how to make a memorial for a pet, the following tips from Kerrin Giovanelli, a family friend who was ten years old when her cat died, may be helpful:

• Create the memorial at the site where your pet died. If that's not possible, choose your pet's favorite spot—next to the fireplace, under a big oak tree, on a kitchen windowsill.

• Mark the spot with flowers or a statue.

• Write your pet's name on a stone or a piece of wood and use it as a marker. If you're creating the memorial inside, you may want to move the marker to an outside location once your pet has been buried.

• Create a keepsake that is small enough to fit in your pocket or under your pillow. (Kerrin opted to needlepoint her cat's name and a cross on a small piece of fabric so that she could carry it with her all the time.)

• Write down some thoughts about your pet either in a journal or in letter form.

• Gather the family around the memorial site and have each family member share a story about your pet.

- Realize that over time the memorial may change. You may want to keep a token reminder at the site and move other objects to a more private place.
- You may want to place flowers on the site on the anniversary of your pet's death, on the day she was born, or on the day you brought her home.

ACTIVITY

CREATING A MEMORY BOOK

Help your child create a scrapbook in honor of your loved one. Use materials and remembrances from around the house to make a simple book that your child will treasure.

STEP 1. For the cover, cut a piece of oaktag into two nine-by-twelve-inch rectangles. (Or you can use a cereal box or cardboard and cover the pieces with wallpaper, fabric, or construction paper.)

STEP 2. Allow your child to decorate the cover—provide photos, markers, paints, crayons, glue, glitter, ribbon.

STEP 3. Let your child pick out some photos of your deceased loved one to include in the book. If there are other keepsakes that you are willing to pass along, provide those as well (pressed flowers, programs from special events, favorite recipes, favorite poems, a birthday or Christmas card, etc.). An older child may want more specific items, such as the obituary from the newspaper or the prayer card from the funeral home.

STEP 4. Help your child piece together her favorite memories of your loved one. Let your child write these stories down or, if your child is too young, dictate the stories to you. Put these down on paper, leaving room for photos and other mementos.

STEP 5. Create a "Remember when . . ." page and ask your child to list some special times she spent with your loved one. (Inside pages can be plain white paper,

construction paper, or lined loose-leaf paper—
whichever your child prefers.)

STEP 6. Leave one page for "favorites" and try to list your
loved one's favorite food, color, song, poem, book,
vacation spot, etc.

STEP 7. Allow your child to draw pictures on the pages,
maybe even creating a portrait of your loved one to
include as an entire page in the book.

STEP 8. Collect all of the pages and use a hole punch to put a
set of two holes along the left edges of the covers
and pages.

STEP 9. Group the pages together in whatever order your
child prefers and use a ribbon or string to tie the
pages and covers together.

ACTIVITY

ACTIVITY

Alternate Memory Makers

A memory book is just one way to create a keepsake of a loved one. Your child may prefer to create something different. Let your child use his imagination, or take ideas from the list below:

Create a memory mobile. Select seashells, pinecones, pictures, trinkets, or any small mementos of a loved one that have special meaning. Tie the items to pieces of yarn cut at various lengths. Tie the other ends of the yarn to the bottom of a clothes hanger. Your child can suspend the mobile from his bedroom ceiling, providing a visible reminder of your loved one.

Create a memory box. This is an especially nice idea if your child has actual items from a loved one that are too big or too bulky to paste into a book. Take a shoe box or buy a small plastic box and allow your child to decorate the outside with paints, stickers, fabric, wallpaper, contact paper, and/or photos. Line the inside with tissue paper, wrapping paper, or fabric. Allow your child to include small items that remind her of your loved one—a special rock, a lapel pin, photos, a prayer book, a pressed flower. Your child can take the box out and look at the items whenever she is missing your loved one.

Create a bookmark. This is an especially simple activity— good for very young children or those who are not as interested in artistic endeavors. Find a favorite photo of your loved one. Have your child glue the photo to a piece of colored paper or cardboard. Let him write your loved one's name, birth year, and death year under the photo (or write it for him). An older child may want to write a poem or include a quote from your loved one's favorite poem. Use clear contact paper to cover the bookmark. Your child can use the bookmark in a favorite book, journal, or prayer book.

ACTIVITY

5

When the Time Is Right: Learning to Start Over

- Can we help our children learn to live again?

- How can we make our kids feel safe?

- How do we set examples of healthy behavior?

- When will our children step out of their grief?

**Do not be afraid of risks! God's strength
is always far more powerful
than your difficulties.**
Pope John Paul II, *Letter to Families*, 1994

In the days immediately following my mother's death, there
was a steady stream of visitors to our home. Many of them
came bearing casseroles and cakes, trays of cold cuts and pots
of soup. It was as though they could keep the grief at bay by
feeding us around the clock, and it was probably one of the
most important things that anyone did for us at that point
in time. It gave us a chance not to think about cooking or
shopping or eating. We sat down and, almost as if by magic,
plates of food appeared before us.

Then our friends and neighbors went back to their old
lives. That was something they couldn't do for us. That was
something we couldn't even do for ourselves. We could never
go back to what was, only forward to a new place that we had
never been to before. When the food stopped arriving and
the flowers started wilting, we were suddenly roused from our
grief to find that we were expected to go on—somehow.

⁓

It is a harsh awakening when you realize that the earth does not stop spinning on its axis just because someone you love dies. People go about their business. Life, for the most part, goes on without missing a beat. You find yourself asking, How can this be? Why isn't everyone weeping? Didn't this life *mean* something? In the midst of that shock and disbelief, it is almost impossible to conceive of going on with your own life.

But when the initial days of official mourning are over, families are faced with that overwhelming reality. Adults go back to work. Children return to school. Eventually, everyone in the family is expected to recreate some version of his or her former life. Despite the fact that society gives the bereaved only a few days to "get over" their grief, it takes much longer than that to plod through the fields of sorrow to a place where the soil is fertile enough to support a new beginning. That's what this fourth grief task is all about: finding a way to move on without forgetting the loved one who is gone.

Children may have an especially difficult time learning to live, laugh, and trust in spite of their grief. They may think that going on with their lives means leaving their loved one behind. They may feel disloyal or cruel. Worse yet, others may make them feel that way. Our job as parents is to help them understand that it is normal and healthy to go on living—and even enjoying life—after the death of a loved one or friend.

We can teach our children that losing one person does not mean that everyone we love will die. We can show them that it's OK to invest our hearts in new relationships. We can help them find the trust that they lost—trust that those around them won't disappear, trust that God is not out to get them, trust that the world is not inherently bad.

According to Donna Schuurman, kids wonder how they can possibly feel good when someone they love is dead. "It's a catch-22. They want to feel better, but you can feel guilty about feeling better. It's a long-term process. Often this is happening at a time when kids are developing in other ways—their bodies are growing, their hormones are changing. That's just a huge additional piece to have to try to figure out, and often they're trying to figure it out alone."

Can we help our children learn to live again?

For many children, the death of a loved one can burn a permanent change onto their very souls. Learning to live again seems like an impossible request. A teenage boy loses his mother to cancer, and now he is supposed to rent a tux for the prom or put on his football uniform for the big game. It may never happen. The wound may be too fresh or too deep to allow him to reach that point quickly. On the other hand, some children may find comfort in doing "normal" things. That is why it is so important not to judge a child's behavior as a sign of his or her concern or lack of concern for the deceased person.

Jennifer Morgan, who talked earlier about her brother's drowning at age fourteen, says that the demands of day-to-day life were still there after Robby's death, and that, in a way, they forced life to go on. "My parents had three other children to provide for. Julie and I still had to go to softball, piano, and ballet. Peter needed to be brought to soccer practice and karate."

Jennifer's story isn't uncommon. Life does go on. Adults and children in grief soon learn that going back to ballet lessons, school, work, or ceramics class is healthier than sitting home alone and crying. The question is how do we help our children get from a place of grief to a place where they feel safe enough to rebuild around their loss.

Schuurman says that the process begins by simply allowing our children to express their feelings. "This is a continually negotiated process. There is not a magical ending point. Ultimately, forcing children to do things or not allowing them to do things doesn't work too well. It goes back to providing the proper environment, the same way you would for a physical wound, because this is an emotional wound. What you do to allow healing will vary depending upon the severity of the wound, from day to day and person to person."

This period of the grief process is the time when a child may feel a different kind of guilt because she is beginning to enjoy life again and is not always focused on the person who has died. It is a time when parents and other adults may expect fears and other symptoms of grief to begin fading, when in reality such symptons remain a very big part of the child's healthy grieving.

For Jennifer Morgan, grief was like a roller-coaster ride. "You refuse to accept that this has happened. You feel depressed, sad, lonely, like it can't get any worse. Then you begin to laugh again and experience feelings of guilt. Why should I be happy if Robby is dead? I'm still grieving, but life continues. I am very happy. I know I have a special guardian angel who looks out for me. I know I will see him again."

So our children may find themselves laughing and happy despite their best efforts to maintain a solemn appearance in memory of the dead family member or friend. And just as quickly they are tossed back into depression over the idea that they could be so cruel as to be happy when a person they love is gone. Guilt takes over and pushes our children's progress back a few steps. Grief doesn't always move forward in a direct and clear path.

As we parents sit on the sidelines and wince for our children every time they beat themselves up over something that's not their fault, we have to remember that all of this is normal. Our kids wouldn't be kids, wouldn't be human, if they didn't feel the same guilt and glee that all of us feel at one time or another. Our job is to let them know that it's OK to be happy, that learning to laugh again does not mean we have stopped loving our dead friend or relative.

How can we make our kids feel safe?

There are no magic potions or secret strategies when it comes to helping children adjust to loss or feel safe enough to trust again. We have to learn to give them a healthy balance of support and private time. From a parent's perspective, however, it can be pretty hard to decide which is needed most when a child is hurting. Our natural instinct makes us want to hug them, hold them tight, tell them everything will be OK.

Even during minor upheavals in my children's lives, I often don't know whether to hover around trying to engage them or to disappear and let them have time alone. It comes back to reading our children. My son, Noah, tends to put on a tough-guy, no-tears facade, pretending he's not hurting or afraid. The reality, we have found, is that he's scared of something and is waiting for us to gently ease into a subject, not through direct questioning but through play and art and casual conversations.

So how does your child respond to different approaches? Does he like to be questioned directly about events? Does she prefer quiet closeness, curled up on your lap for a book? Does he want to retreat to his room one minute and then lash out at you the next for not noticing how much pain he is in? Before we get our backs up or let our tempers flare over what seems to be inconsistent or outright hostile behavior, we can reflect on the ways our children deal with everyday issues. Then, using that knowledge, we can begin to use our familiar parenting strategies to help our children express all the things that are bottled up and waiting to come out.

There is one thing of which we can be sure: Our kids want a safe place to retreat to during the grieving process and a safe place to emerge from when the time comes to move on. We can provide that secure and comfortable haven by making our home a place where no comments or questions are judged harshly or laughed at or ignored. We parents can encourage healthy conversations by listening, being truthful and consistent, and fostering an atmosphere in which our loved one's memory becomes a healthy and happy part of our lives.

It is possible to remember a deceased family member or friend without being morbid. Sharing stories, remembering favorite places or events, hanging up a few special photographs —all of these simple actions go a long way toward helping our kids know that we have not forgotten our loved one.

Grief expert Alan Wolfelt sums it up best in his video *A Teen's View of Grief*: "Normalize but do not minimize." If we can remember those words, we can help our children find a healthy place to plant the seeds of new life.

How do we set examples of healthy behavior?

Once our children have accepted the reality of a loved one's death and have begun the long process of making that reality part of their lives, how do we help them resume the interests and relationships they had before or perhaps even forge new ones?

It will not be easy, but one thing that will make the road smoother is the good example of healthy grief that they witness in us. We can model for our children what to do when they experience a loss. We can let them see us go back to our exercise class or book discussion group. We can invite friends over for dinner. We can begin laughing again. We can show them that life goes on. It is changed, for sure, but it can be happy once again.

We should be aware that throughout their lives our children will continually renegotiate the issues surrounding that loss, especially during adolescence and as they enter into new relationships.

Miriam Klotz, a social worker with Hospice Austin in Texas, says that a child's ability to negotiate successfully depends on whether his grief has been worked through. "Even if a child lost a parent at age five, when he gets to high-school graduation his grief will be recognized at that moment. When he gets married, it will again be recognized. At each developmental stage it will come up. With each kind of cognitive development, children will reprocess the whole thing, given the opportunity, and come to different terms with it."

That's certainly how it has been for me in the changing terrain of grief since my mother's death thirteen years ago. When Noah was born, I felt cheated because of her absence. Every time that I wondered how she handled my sleepless nights as a baby, whether I had colic, or whether she ever felt inadequate, I felt a new surge of anger over the fact that I did not have what so many of my friends had: a mother to talk them through some of the really rough times of early motherhood. When Olivia was born more than three years later, a deep sense of sadness surfaced. In fact, I had my most vivid dreams of my mother only weeks before my daughter was born. I know it was because, on some level, I was grieving again, missing my mother in a new way because she was missing this important milestone in my life and the lives of her grandchildren.

But I am at a place now where I am very aware of this kind of grief. I recognize it, own it, and in some ways enjoy the way it brings back the memory of my mother so vividly.

Our children will go through these kinds of regrieving episodes throughout their lives. It is normal and healthy. We can be available to them any time a major milestone or event is on the horizon, any time our children are experiencing extraordinary burdens or joys. We can let them know it's nothing to be ashamed of and nothing to fear. Tell them to let the feelings in, reflect on what's happening, and find the good that comes from remembering.

When will our children step out of their grief?

Our children cannot move forward if their daily lives are still heavily intertwined with thoughts of a deceased relative or friend. They must come to a clear understanding that they can hold onto the memories of that person and, at the same time, move ahead with the next phase of their lives, whatever and whomever that may include. They do have to take those memories and find an appropriate place for them in their lives.

It is unlikely that our kids will ever feel that the issue of loss is completely resolved. It is key that we parents provide an atmosphere where healing can take place, allowing our children to talk about the deceased loved one if that is what they want, but not forcing them to talk if they prefer to be silent. Providing opportunities for rituals around anniversaries, holidays, and birthdays is also an important part of the process at this stage.

Jennifer Morgan says that the first Christmas after Robby's death was very difficult. There was no Christmas tree, and the family dinner, which was normally hosted at her house, was moved to an aunt's house instead. "It was really awful. I remember being ten, sitting in my aunt's house, all the gifts a kid could want, but feeling this numbness. All the forced smiles were hiding sad faces. Christmas was our favorite time of year, and I wondered if it would ever be the same."

The answer to that, of course, is no, it will never be the same. But eventually it can be happy. Although the first anniversary, birthday, and major holidays after a loved one's death are usually painful and sad, it is important to find ways to commemorate those occasions in positive ways. What was Dad's favorite food? Go to a restaurant and order it. What was Mom's favorite activity? Pile the kids in the car and do it. Getting outside, sharing happy memories, and doing something fun are healthy ways to show kids that they can remember the person who is gone with laughter as well as with tears.

Pediatrician Alan Greene says that people get into the most trouble during the holidays if they force themselves to be happy and refuse to acknowledge who is missing or how the special day has changed. "Take a few minutes right at the beginning of the celebration to say, 'This is really hard. Last year we had Mom with us. This year we don't, and it is really hard.' Acknowledge that at the very beginning. Everybody will feel sad, but then the rest of the holiday can be really uplifting," he says. "If it floats around as this big something missing the entire time, then the holidays become nothing but a drain."

Carol Hyrcza and her family have found unique ways of commemorating her son Peter's life on days that hold special meaning for them. "On June 29, the day Peter died, we go to the cemetery with donuts and chocolate milk, and we sit there and eat. Then we do something fun together," says Carol. "On his birthday, we have people over, and we watch a video of him and have dinner. On Halloween, he gets a pumpkin. This Christmas we brought a Christmas tree to the cemetery."

We can't be afraid to mention our loved one's name or talk about the times we shared. Look through photos, play Grandma's favorite song, bake Mom's special cookie recipe, visit the park Grandpa used to love. Kids will relish the opportunity to remember the loved one who is missing, and they will learn that remembering and commemorating are not signs of weakness but signs of strength and growth.

LEARNING TO MOVE ON

LET YOUR CHILDREN SEE YOU ENGAGING IN FAVORITE HOBBIES, FRIENDSHIPS, AND INTERESTS. Not only will it help your children understand that it is OK for their lives and their happiness to flourish, but it will help you regain some sense of normalcy in your own life as well.

ENCOURAGE—BUT DON'T FORCE—YOUR CHILDREN to resume sports, music, or art. You need to give your children "permission" to return to the things they love even if it is without the person they love. They need to know that you will not be angry with or disappointed in them if they want to go back to Little League or ballet class. On the other hand, we parents must avoid the urge to pressure our kids into something they're not ready to do. If you encourage your child to return to a much-loved activity and he balks at the notion, back off. He will let you know when he is ready.

PROVIDE A SAFE, SECURE, AND STABLE ENVIRONMENT AT HOME. Keep mealtimes the same, and try to eat at least one meal a day together as a family. Be available to your child as much as possible, and continue to keep the same rules around the house. Children need the routine of chores, curfews, family dinners, nightly walks. Whatever it is that made your family run well before your loss can help get things back on track after your loss.

AVOID ADDING NEW STRESSES UNTIL YOUR CHILDREN HAVE ADJUSTED to their loss. It may be financially necessary for a parent to take on a new job after a death in the family. However, if at all possible, parents should avoid making drastic changes in their own lives and the lives of their children. Kids who are coping with the loss of someone close to them will be hard-pressed to make additional adaptations. New jobs that take parents away or require changes in childcare are especially troublesome. The same holds true for moves to new towns or new school districts. Now is the time to keep things as steady and familiar as possible.

ACTIVITY

Marking an Anniversary

The anniversary of a loved one's death can be an especially difficult time, but it doesn't have to be all sorrow and mourning. You can honor your loved one in a way that celebrates his life and lifts your spirit.

HAVE A SPECIAL FAMILY DINNER and serve your loved one's favorite foods. It doesn't matter if they don't necessarily go together—be creative. If your loved one liked pancakes, pasta, and apple pie, then that can be the menu. Don't get stuck on the idea of a formal or fancy affair, unless, of course, that is what your loved one liked. The dinner should reflect your loved one's personality. If you're not up to planning a dinner, go out to your loved one's favorite restaurant—maybe even order her favorite meal in her honor.

> **AT THE DINNER TABLE**, have each person share a favorite memory of your loved one or say a special prayer.

> **AFTER DINNER** (or before) go to a park, museum, or other spot that was a favorite of your loved one, or do something she loved to do—walk in the woods, play miniature golf, go out for ice cream.

Other Anniversary Ideas

OPTION 1. Go to Mass together as a family early in the morning and then go out to breakfast or to the cemetery or all three.

OPTION 2. Release a balloon in your loved one's memory and watch it disappear into the clouds.

OPTION 3. Get a bottle of bubbles and blow your sorrows into the wind.

OPTION 4. Go to your loved one's grave and leave a special stone or some other small token of your affection. Some people like to take this even further. I know one family that combines the anniversary dinner with the cemetery visit and has a graveside picnic. It may seem morbid to some, but to others it is the best way to feel close to their loved one at a very special time. As long as it is done with dignity and respect, there's absolutely nothing wrong with it (unless your cemetery has specific rules against it).

OPTION 5. Gather friends and family and watch videos of your loved one and look through photo albums. Share stories and remember the happy times you had together.

ACTIVITY

6

When the Unthinkable Happens: Guiding Our Children through Traumatic Loss

- **Suicide: Do we have to talk about it?**

- **Homicide: How will our children react?**

- **Rampage killings and other tragedies: Can our children find healing after violence?**

- **Miscarriage, Stillbirth, and Infant Death: Will our children understand?**

- **What should we do when a child is dying?**

- **When is it OK to cut and run?**

Children . . . have an extraordinary capacity to see into the heart of things and to expose sham and humbug for what they are.
Archbishop Desmond Tutu, *The Words of Desmond Tutu*

We had a little boy in our group who wanted everyone to guess how his dad died. The kids were saying, "He drowned in a pool." He said, "Nope." "He shot himself in the head?" Again, he said, "Nope." They were saying all these macabre things and getting a kick out of it because they couldn't guess. It turned out that he hanged himself. The child illustrated it. He pulled at his neck and fell to the ground. The other children just looked at him. He said, "He put a rope around his neck and stood on a chair." They all said, "Why would he do that?" There was silence, and then the boy, who was four years old, said, "Because he didn't know how much we loved him."

—Donna Schuurman, The Dougy Center, Portland, Oregon

✑

Hearing that story made me want to cry. We don't like to think of children talking about death—especially a parent's death—in those terms. A guessing game? That can't be healthy, right? The reality is that making a game of it was how this child was able to deal with his sadness, his fears, and his confusion. He was in a grief support group with his peers, children who had experienced similar tragedies. He knew he was safe, so he let down his guard and said what he felt. He knew that his father felt unloved—not that he didn't love him enough, but that his father didn't comprehend just how much he did love him. That's a pretty healthy understanding for a four-year-old faced with loss by suicide.

Not all children will cope so well, and often that is not through any fault of their own. According to Donna Schuurman, the stigma attached to certain kinds of deaths can cause additional stress for children in grief. "Some complications make grief more difficult. It has to do with how society views suicides, or how society views homicides, and how the family has to deal with the dragged-out process: the media, the legal system, the sense of unfairness of things, the closure of a trial. It can go on for years."

Suicide: Do we have to talk about it?

When I was doing the research for this book, I traveled around the Internet, stopping in on Web pages run by suicide hotlines and prevention organizations as well as much more personal sites put up by family members struggling with the aftermath of a loved one's suicide. Some of them were painfully honest; all of them were heartbreaking. No one wants to talk about suicide—but we have to. It's out there. It's taking our children in increasing numbers. It is devastating those who are left behind.

According to the National Center for Suicide Statistics, someone attempts suicide every forty-two seconds. Someone dies by suicide every seventeen minutes. As if those statistics aren't sobering enough, here are some more: According to the American Academy of Child and Adolescent Psychiatry, suicide is the third leading cause of death for fifteen- to twenty-four-year-olds and the sixth leading cause of death for five- to fourteen-year-olds. And those numbers are on the rise.

Some of the experts I spoke with said that death by suicide, homicide, and AIDS are among those most likely to be hidden from children. And yet children almost always know the real reason for a loved one's death. What they don't always understand is why everyone is being so hush-hush about it. It makes them feel as though there is something to be ashamed of. It adds to their guilt, and it can disrupt the healthy grieving that needs to take place.

Grief therapist Linda Goldman has written a book on the subject, *Bart Speaks Out: Breaking the Silence on Suicide.* On her Web site she says that we must "explore the topic of suicide openly if we are to break through the barriers of shame and secrecy that accompany this topic and create fertile ground for the resolution of this complicated grief situation."

She says that suicide, homicide, AIDS, violence, and abuse create traumatic emotional issues that keep the child from the "normal flow" of grief. "So often a child cannot say that their special person died because they would have to say how that person died," she says. Goldman refers to these unresolved issues as "frozen blocks of time" and says that they create "a wall of ice between the child and his or her grief."

As difficult as the subject is, we parents can find ways to talk honestly about suicide. Children who lose a loved one to suicide are likely to be confused, guilty, embarrassed, or in denial. We can help by telling them in simple and caring ways what has happened. Answer questions openly but don't go into too much detail. Explain that the person who died had an illness of the mind. Don't be judgmental or get into the morality of suicide. Be sure the child knows that the person who died loved him and that he is in no way responsible for what happened. You and your child are likely to benefit from talking to other survivors, so be sure to contact a suicide support organization for additional assistance (see "Resources for Healing").

Homicide: How will our children react?

Sonora Thomas was thirteen when her older sister, Eliza, was one of four teens brutally murdered in Austin, Texas, in what has come to be known as "The Yogurt Shop Murders." She says that it was not until the arrest of her sister's alleged killers eight years later that she began to feel a sense of closure. Seeing the men in a courtroom was a turning point in her grief. "I realized that there are actual people who did this and that this was really part of my life. These [defendants] were only a few years older than me, and they were younger than my sister."

Sonora says that people did not know what to say to her after her sister's murder. Most people avoided the subject completely. The one person who helped her, she recalls, was a teacher who knew her sister. He simply came up to her and said how sorry he was and that he couldn't believe what had happened. "I wanted that acknowledgment, anything that would take me to the present," she says. One of those things was the comfort of being in church. "I am not Catholic, but I went to the Catholic church near my house many times. I would just sit there and cry and cry and pray and pray. I didn't know where else to go."

Something like a homicide can do more than instill a deep sense of grief. It can also cause fears to well up, especially if the murder occurred at or near the child's home—as it did in Sonora's case.

"That place was only five blocks from my house," she says. "I spent hours there. That's my neighborhood. It's so violating. Even now I have a hard time going out at night. I have become hyperaware of things."

We parents who are comforting children who have suffered a loss due to homicide or suicide should keep in mind the additional complications that come along with this kind of grief. There will be more fears, more guilt, more confusion. It's hard to lose a loved one regardless of the circumstances. When you pile brutality or other types of violence on top of that loss, it can drive children deep into themselves or cause them to lash out at those around them.

Talk as honestly as you can about what has happened, but don't allow children to get caught up in gory details and sensational news reports. Be aware that others will likely be talking as well, maybe even pointing fingers and whispering. All of this will be an incredible burden for your children. You don't want to lie or keep basic information from them, but at the same time you do want to shield them from unnecessary harm. You must strike a delicate balance, one that is likely to be toppled by even the most minor glitch. Be prepared for extreme behaviors and emotions. This is a time to consider contacting a grief support group or counselor who specializes in homicide so that your children have a safe place to talk about what they're feeling.

Rampage killings and other tragedies: Can our children find healing after violence?

My father-in-law called me early on September 11, 2001, and asked if I had turned on the news that morning. I hadn't. When he told me that both towers of the World Trade Center had been hit by planes, I couldn't even begin to comprehend what was happening. I clicked on the television as I finished talking to him, watching in horror as flames and smoke billowed from the familiar buildings.

Despite that I had spent almost two years researching and writing this book, I was dumbfounded by the prospect of telling Noah about what had happened. We had told him all about those towers, about their 110 stories, about how both his dad and I had been in them and looked down from the amazing height. We had promised him that we would take him there on a future visit to see his grandmother in Manhattan. Now, as they stood there bleeding debris and humanity onto the streets below, I was sickened by the idea of talking to him about something so horrific and so far beyond any kind of explanation.

I let him see a brief glimpse of the buildings on fire before turning off the television to take him to art class. I knew he might hear others talking about it, so I thought it best for him to hear this news from someone he trusts. I gingerly told him that some "bad people" had caused an explosion in the towers, choosing to leave the planes out of it so as not to cause him to rethink his dream of becoming a pilot when he grows up. He asked a few questions about where the bad people were and why they would do this, but then let it drop.

When he got out of art class and we arrived back home, I told him that the towers were gone, that they fell down because of the explosion inside. He absorbed it all without appearing too upset, but later that day he asked if the "bad people" might knock down our house; I reassured him that they would not. When he made a logical leap—at least for a four-year-old—and worried that they might knock down his grandmother's apartment building in New York City, I told him he was safe and that no one was going to hurt him or the people he loved. All the while I found myself wondering if I was telling him a lie.

Although my husband and I restricted our television viewing over the next few days, being sure that he never once saw the image of the second plane actually hitting—and disappearing into—the building, we could tell that Noah was troubled by what he knew and what he sensed in us. He was edgier and angrier. I couldn't imagine what it must have been like for the children who actually witnessed the terrorist attack or, even worse, lost a parent or loved one in the tragedy.

For those children, the shock and grief that followed were sure to be anything but typical. In fact, some experts in the immediate aftermath of the attack said that they weren't sure if these children would experience grief in its usual patterns at all. Although the World Trade Center and Pentagon attacks were unique due to the number of people killed and the way in which they died, they are by no means the only types of violent incidents that affect children in our society. Unfortunately, the cycle of violence seems to reach out and grab large numbers of our young people in one way or another on a fairly regular basis.

Too often in recent times we have watched the frightening images on TV as children are led—or carried on stretchers—away from their schools after a shooting rampage. Littleton, Springfield, Jonesboro, Paducah, Conyers, Pearl, Edinboro—

and those are just the big ones. There seems to be an endless
supply of people disturbed enough to take preschoolers
hostage, open fire in an office complex, plant bombs in a
federal building.

Some children are right there, wounded or watching a
best friend bleed to death. Others see the images on television
and fear deep down that it could just as easily have been their
schools, their friends, their lives.

Children who are directly impacted by such tragedies
have to deal with a kind of grief that most of us cannot
imagine. Schools should be places of safety, learning, and
fun. How do children ever return to their studies and move
past the pain?

At the Ferncliff Presbyterian Camp and Conference
Center in Little Rock, Arkansas, ministers and counselors set
out to help the children whose lives were touched by the
school shooting in nearby Jonesboro. What began as a local
effort soon developed into an international program to
help children impacted by violence of all kinds—school
shootings, war, gang activity.

David Gill, a Presbyterian minister and executive director
of Ferncliff, says that the children in his program need to
move beyond the deep grief of the initial experience. They
have an incredible need to talk, to write, and to think about
what happened to them.

"We were in uncharted territory," he says. "Our
philosophy going into this was that the typical church camp
experience—being close to nature, forming community,

recreation, worship, and reflection—are healing things, so why not take those same components and infuse them with special programs?" The result was a series of camps to help children deal with the aftermath of violence. One camp, Connection 2000, spawned a national effort—TOUCH (Teens Offering Understanding, Caring, Healing)—to connect children who are dealing with this unusual kind of grief and help them on the road to healing.

"The kids said that they want to move from being victims to being leaders," says Gill. "They want to help others. They said they don't want to be treated like broken, fragile people, but instead they want to look at how this experience can make them stronger."

According to *Best Practices of Youth Violence Prevention,* a sourcebook put out by the National Center for Injury Prevention and Control, the homicide rate for young people in the United States is the highest among developing countries. More than 3,700 children younger than nineteen years of age died a violent death in 1997 alone. Homicide is the second leading cause of death among fifteen- to twenty-four-year-olds and the fourth leading cause of death among one- to fourteen-year-olds. In the inner cities, where gang violence has become all too common, homicide is the leading cause of death among African American males between the ages of fifteen and twenty-four.

In most cases, we parents cannot begin to understand the lure of gangs. In every city there are groups actively fighting it and trying to educate our young people about the inherent dangers involved in this lifestyle. But the bottom line is that gangs are not going away any time soon. What we parents can do is try to be present for our kids in a very strong way. They need to know that they are safe, loved, valued, and respected.

Children who have been directly affected by gang violence and other violent deaths are going to have bouts of grief and mourning that are foreign to many of the adults around them. This is a case where peer support and even peer counseling can offer a kind of outlet for pent-up emotions that parents simply cannot provide.

A key point to remember when dealing with children who are experiencing this kind of grief is that they were not blank slates when the violence occurred. Some may have been stinging from their parents' recent divorce; others may have been abused; still others may be caught in drug addiction. When we start digging down into their grief and their raw emotions, it's hard to know if the volcanoes that are erupting are due strictly to the violence they experienced or to the other losses and problems they deal with every day. This is true for any child in grief. Their losses will be compounded by any other losses or problems in their lives.

Even after kids have dealt with the initial shock of their experiences, feelings of grief will come back to them in more muted tones over the months and years that follow.

Donna Schuurman says that such grief is part of a lifelong process because any major loss is woven into the fabric of our beings. She pointed to the 1999 massacre at Columbine High

School in Littleton, Colorado. "At Columbine, when school started up again, people there talked about how they painted the library and moved it, saying, 'We survived.' If you weren't directly impacted, you may be able to do that a lot easier than somebody whose brother was killed. For those kids, life will never be the same. Everything is different."

This statement is true of just about every major loss children face. Everything is different. The losses will shape them, color them, maybe even change their futures. When the grief becomes less intense, and the mourning is over, the death will still be there, residing in the recesses of their hearts and minds. It may change their perceptions of the world, of God, of family, and of themselves. And it will stay with them forever.

Not all violent deaths will be on par with Columbine, but for the child who witnesses the violent death of a loved one or friend, the size and scope don't really matter. If a child sees her father die in a gruesome car crash or witnesses her sibling being beaten to death, it will be hard for her to get beyond those vivid images. Nightmares and extreme fears are likely to set in. A child may be afraid to get in a car for fear that she will die in a crash or to let her surviving parent drive a car for similar reasons. If the death was at the hands of someone else, there may be fantasies of revenge.

Witnessing a violent death adds extra weight to the already heavy load that grief piles on the shoulders of our children. This may be a case where no amount of hugging and listening will calm their fears. Professional counseling and ongoing support through a grief organization can help start the healing process. In these cases, they are a must.

Miscarriage, stillbirth, and infant death: Will our children understand?

Death is not an easy concept for children to grasp, and the death of a baby is especially difficult for little ones to understand. A child is going to ask questions, either out loud at the dinner table or in the silence of his or her own inner world: *How can a baby die? If a baby can die, then I can die. Did I cause the baby's death?*

When I lost a baby through miscarriage, my son was only one and a half years old. He was too young to understand what was happening. In fact, he was too young to even know that I was pregnant. He did know that Mommy was crying a lot and that we were running from one doctor's office to another. He was with us when the midwife couldn't find the heartbeat, when the ultrasound technician confirmed what we already suspected, when we sat in a long line at the hospital arranging the details of what had to be done. He saw my tears and heard my sobbing, but he was still too young to comprehend why.

When I became pregnant again, my husband and I were very careful of what Noah knew and when he knew it. We didn't tell him about the baby until we had heard the heartbeat. Even up until the day Olivia was born we were careful to phrase things in ways that wouldn't harm him if something horrible were to happen. Every time we told him not to bang into Mommy's belly or jump on Mommy unexpectedly, we worried that if something happened to our unborn baby he would hold himself responsible. And that wasn't just paranoia.

He had, on more than on occasion, expressed concern that he would do something and "the baby would never come out." So children do internalize the things they hear and see. When it comes to miscarriage, stillbirth, or infant death, we have to talk to our children about the sad reality and the fact that nobody is to blame.

Children need to hear that they had no part in the tragedy. They need to know that sometimes babies are not healthy enough or strong enough to make it to birth, that sometimes they have problems with their hearts or their lungs or any number of other ailments that cause them to die when they should be staring wide-eyed at a whole new world.

Don't be surprised if very young children become more clingy or fearful after the death of an unborn baby or infant. This is a scary thing for everyone involved, and children will feel the effects of such a loss just as their parents do—perhaps not to the same degree, of course, but there will be pain and sadness. Pretending it didn't happen or trying to act as though it is not a big deal doesn't do anyone any good, least of all the children. Acting as though it is not upsetting to lose a child will only add to the surviving child's insecurities and fears: *Would Mommy and Daddy be upset if something happened to me? Isn't it sad when a baby dies?* Simply talk in terms children can understand, be prepared for hard questions, and be willing to cry together.

Family therapy and grief support organizations can be especially helpful to families dealing with the loss of an infant. Don't be afraid to ask for help.

What should we do when a child is dying?

How do you tell a little girl that she has only a few short weeks to live? How do you answer her questions and calm her fears when you have so many of your own to deal with? Once again, children themselves often provide the comfort and prepare the way for us. They can be wise and courageous— if we let them speak their minds.

Mercy Sister Judith Carron, a chaplain at Cardinal Glennon Children's Hospital in St. Louis, remembers the first child who asked her point blank if she was going to die. Her name was Andrea, a bright little eight-year-old girl with congestive heart failure. "I turned the question back to her so I could have a better understanding of what she understood. I asked her if she thought she was going to die. She said she did. I said, 'Andrea, I think you are going to die. We don't know when.' She said she was afraid of being alone. The hospital was noisy, and people kept shutting her door. She didn't like that because it scared her. She was afraid of the dark, and she was afraid of the machines."

Andrea was one of those children who wanted to talk about dying and who was lucky enough to find someone to listen. Her heart was failing, but her spirit was strong. She was seeking reconciliation before her death, and Sister Carron helped her find it.

"She asked me if God was going to be mad at her because she had had a fight with her sister before she went to the hospital," says Sister Carron. "She really wanted to connect with her sister, but they lived a distance away. I suggested that she draw a picture and write a card to her sister because children can express so much through art." Andrea made a card for her sister, telling her how sorry she was for the fight they had. It gave her the peace of mind she needed.

Sister Carron also asked Andrea if there was anything that she wanted. Andrea asked for a make-up kit, complete with lipstick and powder. "Andrea was pretty bluish because of her lack of oxygen. I had a sense she was putting on a new face. It was as though she was preparing herself for meeting God," Sister Carron recalls. "She died a very peaceful death. We made sure she wasn't alone, that she wasn't in the dark."

Andrea may seem to be a rare child, not only facing her own death but actually preparing for it. Then again, according to Sister Carron, children are better equipped than we suspect for handling this kind of overwhelming tragedy. Even when children have not been told that they are dying, there are clues that they may understand more than they let on.

One boy told his mother about a recurring dream: He was drowning and trying to come up for air. Every time he tried to come up, he went back under the water. Once the mother got up the courage to ask her son what the dream meant to him, a conversation about death evolved naturally.

"I don't think there is one way to help a child understand he is dying. It is important to try to assess where the child is, to listen to his questions. You don't just say, 'You're dying,'" says Sister Carron, who has spent twenty years working with children at Cardinal Glennon. "Some children will tell you something through art and language and symbols. They don't always tell you directly."

Another little boy who was diagnosed with leukemia drew a picture of a body of water with lots of waves. A helicopter with a big hook hanging from it hovered over the water. Bobbing around in the waves was a little boat with a person in it. Sister Carron asked the boy about the picture. Not surprisingly, he said that he was the person in the boat and that he wanted to be rescued by the helicopter. The picture opened the door to a deeper discussion about his leukemia.

Emma Duke was only twenty-seven months old when she was diagnosed with cancer. She was four years old when she died. During those intervening years, Emma underwent treatment upon treatment and was always told the truth about what was happening to her. Her mom, Kathy, says that through it all Emma held onto the hope that when she was well enough the family would go to Disneyland.

"By the time she got off treatment, she was so weak and so sick. We were trying to build her up, but she relapsed,"

Kathy says. Despite her condition, Emma continued to hope, saying, "Disneyland soon." But Disneyland never happened for Emma. Her treatments made her weak and even caused her to lose her hearing.

"We didn't realize we were going to lose contact with her in such a profound way. It was real hard to communicate. She was in such bad shape," Kathy says. "At the very end I finally whispered to her, 'You don't have to be miserable. You can go if you need to.' She grabbed my hand and said, 'I love you, Mom.'"

At the same time Emma was confronting her own death, her brother, Joseph, was dealing with the inevitable loss of his sister. Kathy says that the two were very close and that Joe adored his little sister. He was with Emma every step of the way and was devastated by her death.

The siblings of children who die from cancer or other long-term illnesses suffer their own kind of special grief, a grief that in some ways starts before the death actually occurs. Often it is grief over a childhood disrupted or lost, grief over the loss of a parent's attention, grief over the loss of an active playmate and partner, or grief over the loss of the life they once knew.

Sister Carron says that parents are often torn between the sick child and the healthy children, and they tend to give more attention to the sick child. "It's important for parents to spend some alone time with the well children, especially with younger children, although teenagers will feel the absence of a mother as well."

Parents can look for support through church and community organizations as well as among family members and friends. The well child may benefit from something as simple as a trip with Mom or Dad to the hospital cafeteria or the nearest McDonald's. Remember, though, that kids in this kind of situation will often be envious of the attention the sick child is getting. That doesn't make them bad kids. It makes them normal.

After the death of a child, siblings may have additional guilt, anger, questions, and fears. Funeral director Peter Assumma says that when he talks to siblings, he first makes sure that they understand how extraordinary the situation is. For most kids, he says, the biggest fear is that they are going to die as well. "We need to be able to take that fear away from that child. We need to help that child recognize that it is so extraordinary for a child to die."

Assumma also has found that parents' typical reaction is to shield their surviving children from the death of a sibling. In his experience, however, as soon as a child is a toddler he is old enough to be included in the events surrounding a brother's or sister's death.

"You want the child to understand that a family deals with everything together—good and bad," he says. "Children should not be prevented from being a part of it and really should play a role in it if they are old enough to have known their brother or a sister."

If the deceased child had a favorite toy, let a little brother leave that toy in the casket with his sister. If he wants to be part of the funeral Mass or memorial service, find a way to make that happen—as altar server, lector, or as a hand-holding companion for Mom or Dad.

When is it OK to cut and run?

We've talked a lot about honesty and about sharing facts with our children, but sometimes we have to know when our children need protection more than they need information.

I am very open with my son, Noah, when it comes to things that are going on in the world. He is very inquisitive, always asking questions and jumping into conversations that I have with my husband. But once in a while I have to turn off the television in the middle of a newscast or stop a conversation before he hears something that is just too much for his young mind to bear.

Recently, while Noah was helping his grandpa check e-mail and stock reports on the computer, my father was startled by a story on the Internet: Police said a mother in Houston had apparently drowned her five children, one by one, and then called her husband and the police. My father read the headline for those of us in the next room. "Don't say anything else," I called out, knowing that this information would scare Noah needlessly. Mothers killing children: that would leave him with way too much to think about when he's lying in the dark trying to go to sleep.

There are times for full disclosure, and there are times to speak in whispers. That's how I felt the day Timothy

McVeigh was executed. I turned on the news to see what was happening. A list of names was rolling by on the screen. Noah looked up and said something about movie credits, assuming it was the end of a show. I began to explain that the names were those of people who had been killed by a very bad man, a man who was going to be punished that morning. I told him how some of the people who died were little babies like his sister, some not even born yet. Others were like Mommy and Daddy and Grandpa and Grandma. We said a quick prayer for them and watched in silence.

I could see all of this registering on Noah's face. He asked how they were killed. I ignored his question. He asked how they were going to punish the bad man. I turned off the TV and told him that the man was going to be locked up for the rest of his life. So I went against my own advice and told a lie, albeit a white one, but a lie nonetheless. The thing is, after thinking about it and discussing it with my husband, I would tell the same white lie again.

My son didn't know who Timothy McVeigh was. He didn't know the people who died in the bombing. He doesn't read or go to a school where it would have been discussed. He had no connection to or knowledge of this event whatsoever. There was no way I could explain a state-ordered execution to an extremely bright and inquisitive four-year-old without getting into the gory details. He would have obsessed over it for days, if not weeks. He would have wanted to know how they killed him, and I would have had to tell him that they did it with injections, needles, shots. He would have immediately related that to the shots he gets at the doctor's office.

Some experts might very well disagree with my approach. But, knowing my son the way I do, I used my judgment during the split second I had to come up with an answer. Noah may understand death—to the degree that a four-year-old can understand—but he is not ready to grasp the concept of our government killing someone as punishment. I'm not even

DEALING WITH DIFFICULT CIRCUMSTANCES

LOOK AT THE DEATH THROUGH YOUR CHILD'S EYES. How will it change her life? Has she been given enough information to make sense of what is happening? Will this loss change her daily routine? Will it change everything as she knows it? Is she wondering who is going to take care of her or where she is going to live? Is she afraid that something similar is going to happen to her parents, her siblings, herself? Imagine being a child again and dealing with the loss of someone you love. What would you need most?

ANSWER QUESTIONS TRUTHFULLY, BUT WITHOUT GORY DETAIL. If a child's grandfather died of cancer and the child was not aware of it prior to the death, now is not the time to talk about the details of the disease. Simply tell the child that Grandpa's heart (liver, lungs, brain, etc.) stopped working the way it should. If your child has additional questions, answer them as ready to grasp that. I found no compelling reason to burden him with information that could do more harm than good at this point in his life. So I found a shade of gray in the midst of all the black and white advice I've been sharing.

You know your children. You love your children. Let those two things be your guide as you help your children deal with the tragedies that befall them. You are the expert when it comes to what your own children can handle.

directly as possible. If a child's sibling died in a car crash, there is no need to talk about everything leading up to the death. Simply talk about the fact that sometimes there are accidents and that the doctors tried to save her brother (sister, father, friend, etc.) but his body was too badly hurt.

EXPECT NEW FEARS TO SPRING FROM THIS EVENT and the information you provide. Worries about getting a disease, dying in a car crash, being in a shooting are likely to surface, depending on the death and the age of your child.

EXPECT SOME QUESTIONS THAT YOU WILL NOT BE ABLE TO ANSWER. If a child wants to know why his uncle killed himself, you will probably not be able to provide a pat

(continued)

answer. The same holds true for other violent deaths that defy logic. When these kinds of questions arise, talk to your child honestly. Don't be afraid to say that you don't have an answer. Contact a support group or clergy member to explore the question and find a resolution to your child's concerns.

KNOW WHEN TO SHIELD YOUR CHILDREN FROM HARMFUL NEWS that does not affect them directly. Does your child need to hear about every school shooting, every tornado, and every madman who walks into an office building and opens fire? Absolutely not. This is a situation where your child's age should determine what you tell her. If a child is old enough to hear about the event through schoolmates or newspapers, then by all means talk about it. Use your own judgment and discretion—but if you do choose to discuss an especially alarming death with your child, be prepared to help her wade through the scary information.

GET YOUR CHILDREN ONE-ON-ONE COUNSELING OR GROUP SUPPORT to help them through their grief. Let your children know that it is healthy and beneficial to talk to others, especially professionals, about what they are feeling. If you are grieving as well, you can set a good example by joining a grief support group or seeking a counselor's assistance. Your attitude toward outside help will directly influence your children's attitudes.

Acting On Your Feelings

ACTIVITY

We can help our children move through grief—and maybe even help ourselves along the way—if we can show them how to turn their inward sorrow into outward action. This is not something you can do with a child who is deep in the initial throes of grief, but rather it is something that your child will progress toward as he integrates his feelings of grief into the rest of his life. By becoming an "activist" of sorts, your child will learn how something sad can spark something positive.

ACTION 1. If your child's deceased loved one was elderly, ask if he would like to volunteer some of his time at a local nursing home or hospital. Visit patients who don't have family around. Sing songs together at the holidays. Read a book to someone who can no longer read for herself. It may take some initial prodding, but it is likely to be an experience your child will never forget.

ACTION 2. Visit a children's ward or children's hospital. Call a hospital and see if it would be OK for your child to bring some colorful balloons, a book for story time, some puppets for a show, or some paper and crayons for arts and crafts. You'll be amazed at how something so simple can be so powerful. Watch the faces light up—theirs and yours!

ACTION 3. Help your child find an organization dedicated to your loved one's favorite cause or to a cause that is somehow related to his or her death. Encourage

ACTIVITY

your child to join a fund-raising walk for AIDS or breast cancer research. Suggest that she volunteer her time with the American Cancer Society, the American Heart Association, the American Diabetes Association, or another appropriate group. Write letters, raise money, donate time.

ACTION 4. Once your child has worked through some of his own grief issues, see if he would like to become a peer counselor. Many local grief programs train young people to help others their own age.

ACTION 5. Help your child research topics related to your loved one's death. He may feel empowered by this new information (e.g., using sunblock to ward off skin cancer, eating right to prevent colon cancer, exercising to keep your heart healthy, avoiding cigarettes to prevent lung cancer, knowing the dangers of drinking and driving).

7

Watch, Listen, and Learn: Respecting Our Children's Grief

- **What can we learn from our children's grief?**

- **What do children hear?**

- **How does grief evolve?**

- **Are we open or closed to our children?**

- **What do we say?**

O divine Master, grant that I may not so much seek to be consoled as to console, to be understood as to understand, to be loved as to love.

St. Francis of Assisi

When we moved our family across the country from Austin, Texas, to Delmar, New York, one of our biggest concerns was for Noah. He had recently begun attending a Montessori school he absolutely loved and had successfully adjusted to a new baby sister. Now we were asking him to adjust again—to a new town, a new climate, another new school, new friends, new everything.

At first he didn't seem to comprehend the finality of the move. He thought we were going back to Austin, that our house would be there waiting for us even though it had a new owner, that this journey was just an extended vacation. When reality set in, the problems began. There wasn't anything serious, but there were definite behavior changes. We could see it in the way he interacted with us, with his sister, Olivia, and with the kids in his new school. He got quieter. He wanted to be alone more often. He seemed angrier.

We did our best to help him make this monumental adjustment. We painted his bedroom the exact same shade of blue as his bedroom in Austin. He hung up some of the same decorations. We enrolled him in the local Montessori school within weeks of our arrival. We talked about our old home and his old school often. We even filled in a journal about moving. This gave him a chance to list the best things about his old home and his new home and the worst things about both places. The exercise allowed him to see that everything about Austin wasn't wonderful and that everything about Delmar wasn't awful.

Six months later his adjustment is complete. He loves his new school, his new room, and the snow that piled up around our doors and windows during the winter. He's going to play with a new friend this afternoon and is taking an art class as I write this. He loves "our" museum and "our" farm. He still talks about Austin sometimes, but usually it involves a vacation there to see his cousins. Because we let him run through the gamut of emotions—sadness, anger, disappointment, and, finally, joy—Noah has been able to adjust to his new life on his own schedule. When he was upset, we acknowledged that this was a very difficult thing to go through. When he was sad, we honored it but reminded him that soon our new house would feel like home. We learned that we couldn't force anything. We had to take our cues from him.

❧

Just as we allowed Noah to lead the way through his grief over losing the only home he knew, we parents can take cues from our children when they are grieving the death of someone close to them. We can respect their feelings, accept their reactions, and encourage their healing. By putting aside our preconceived notions of what grief should be like, we allow our children to be our teachers. With our permission, they will open up to us, trust us, and maybe even help us a little along the way.

Every child experiences death differently. Unique personality traits, family upbringing, and support systems color the ways they react. When Gregory Floyd's six-year-old son, John Paul, was hit by a car in front of his house, it set in motion a long journey for Gregory, his wife, Maureen, and their six surviving children. There were good-byes at John Paul's hospital bed, good-byes at the funeral and burial, good-byes as each child came to terms with how their brother's death impacted their everyday life at home. Through it all, the Floyds were careful to create an environment in which their children felt free to express their feelings.

"We needed to constantly convey to them that there is no such thing as right or wrong feelings, that it's OK to feel angry, it's OK to feel sad, it's OK to feel happy about Johnny," says Gregory, who recalls how his children would want to paint at an easel, go out for ice cream, and weep for their dead brother all in the span of a half hour.

The Floyds honored their children's feelings and reactions, recognizing that each of them had to grieve in ways they were comfortable with. David, who survived being hit by the same car as John Paul, said that he saw his brother "everywhere." No matter where he looked, he was confronted with his brother's absence. Therese, who Gregory says has a "Miss Fix-It" personality, said at one point that she hated "all this grief." She couldn't deal with the fact that she was unable to make things better. The Floyds' eldest son, Gregory, came to his parents and said that he felt bad because he didn't have as much sorrow as his mother and father.

"We told him, 'You're not supposed to feel a parent's grief because you're not a parent. You've got a brother-sized grief. You've got enough grief to deal with. You don't need to deal with the grief that Mommy and Daddy are feeling.' He got set free by that."

What can we learn from our children's grief?

Gregory and Maureen also realized early on that their children were looking to them for cues. They knew they had to exhibit behavior that would allow their children to express their own grief in healthy ways. And, when their grief started to take them too deep into themselves, their children were there to pull them back from the depths.

"By being their own vulnerable, charming, needy selves, they helped us immensely," Gregory recalls. "During that first week, I remember standing in the hallway greeting people and mentally feeling like I'm falling off a cliff, and I can't even reach the bottom and crash. I'm just free-falling endlessly, and then I feel this little tug on my thigh, and it's my daughter Susanna, and I get called back to life because there's a little child here who needs me. That was how God used them to draw us out of ourselves, because children are essentially needy."

He says that "obedience to the everyday"—getting the kids dressed, making them breakfast, saying their prayers, and tucking them in at night—forced the family to move forward. The same can be true for anyone dealing with grief. A return to "normal" life helps take our children away from their grief for brief moments throughout the day. A routine provides a framework. If their daily needs are being met—food, clothes, sleep, comfort—children are more likely to begin to heal emotionally and spiritually. And, by staying involved in their daily routines, we put ourselves in the position of being available to them whenever a scary thought or question comes up.

I work at home, so except for Noah's short afternoon school session, he and Olivia are with me all day, every day. Often his questions and concerns about moving would come up in unexpected ways, like the time we were cooking pancakes, and he said, "This is the first time we're having pancakes—in this house." I knew that he was thinking about his old life in Austin. It allowed me to join in the reminiscing and at the same time talk about how exciting it was to be doing this for the first time in our new home. It was through our ordinary activities that he expressed his extraordinary worries and fears. Children are not going to make appointments to sit down and talk frankly about their concerns. They are going to see something that sparks a question, eat something that brings back a memory, go somewhere that causes them to break into tears—or into laughter. If we can be there with them, we can be there for them.

My young sister-in-law, Allison Martin, was ten years old when she came across a story in *Good Housekeeping* of a one-year-old boy who suffocated after getting tangled in his crib sheet. Although it affected her deeply, she initially didn't say anything to her parents about it. A few weeks later, during the course of a conversation, she mentioned something to her mother about sheets being dangerous. My mother-in-law, Mary Ann Poust, says that at first she scoffed at the idea, but Allison said she would prove her point and came back with the article in hand.

"I was surprised at what I read, but more surprised at her interest and knowledge," says Mary Ann. "That opened the discussions as to how badly she felt for that family and how sad she was that the child had died. To help her feel that she could help in some way, I suggested that she write to the mother expressing sympathy and making a contribution to the foundation they had set up."

Allison did just that, making a twenty-five-dollar donation that would go toward a playground the family was building at the public school their little boy would have attended. But it didn't end there. Allison and the child's mother continued to correspond from time to time, and Allison even made a presentation on the crib sheet issue at her school. When the playground was dedicated in June 1999, Allison and her parents made the drive from Manhattan to Norwood, Massachusetts, for the event. The family even singled Allison out during the event, telling everyone there how much she had helped the grieving mother.

Mary Ann says that she thinks the situation had such a dramatic impact on Allison because it made her realize that sometimes bad things happen even when you're in a situation that's considered safe. "The baby was in his own home, his own room, and his own bed," she says. "His mother was in the house, taking care of him. And yet he died. Although she never articulated it in that way, I think that was an awakening for Allison, and a frightening one. I think her activism was a way of dealing with it."

And so there we have a perfect example of how a child can be moved to great lengths by the death of someone she doesn't even know. Her parents could have told her to forget about it. They could have said it was sad but not her problem. They certainly could have said that it was too far to drive to another state for a playground dedication. But they didn't. They honored their daughter's feelings, and she responded by moving through her initial reaction to a place where she could use her concern to comfort a mother in grief and educate others. That is what happens when parents watch, listen, and learn.

What do children hear?

Michaelene Mundy—a teacher, mother, counselor, and author—says that parents can look for the "simple insights" children offer into how they understand death and grief. If we parents are awake to those comments, we can take them to the next level by helping our children find the answers to their questions.

"Children deserve our respect," Mundy says. "My main admonition to parents, teachers, and caregivers is to communicate—that doesn't mean just talk, but listen carefully to what a child is saying. Children are very literal, so it's important to be aware of what we say to our children. They are listening to what is said around them and are interpreting in the best way they know how with their limited experience."

Mundy recalls that when her son Michael was three years old, he believed her deceased father lived in the attic. He had heard her speak of someone being "up in heaven" and also understood that heaven was not a place you could visit. In his preschool mind he put two and two together: The entrance to the attic was a square hole "up" in the ceiling. Nobody ever went there, but he knew it existed. In his mind, that was where his grandfather must be.

Think about even the most basic ways that our children can misinterpret what we say. Noah's mind starts whirring with wonder when I say that I'm going to "throw" a load of wash in or "run" to the store. "The store is too far away," he'll say, and I end up in a ridiculously long discussion about the simplest things. The same holds true for children who are trying to understand death. What seems like a simple statement to us can be rife with strange images to a child.

Father Terence Curley, a grief expert and the author of *The Ministry of Consolation: A Parish Guide for Comforting the Bereaved*, says that euphemisms and attempts to shield children from the truth can add to a child's emotional confusion.

"Our language is important in the way we talk about death with the child," says Father Curley. "Children can easily misinterpret our abstractions. For example, telling a child that someone was so good that God took them could bring about real problems. In the child's view this could mean that if you're really good God is going to take you too. This can be frightening and certainly shapes the child's image of God." The key is honesty. The truth is always best, no matter how painful.

How does grief evolve?

In the beginning, a child's grief can seem overwhelming for us parents to deal with. But remember: This too will pass, though it will not pass quickly. Just as we cannot teach our children all there is to know about right and wrong in one night, we cannot hope to explain death, grief, mourning, resurrection, and survival in one sitting. Over the months and years ahead, questions will continue to come up. It's normal and healthy. Experts call it "regrieving," but for most of us it's simply called life.

A child's graduation comes along, and he thinks about how his mom would have been so proud. A daughter prepares to get married, and she cries over the fact that her dad is not there to walk her down the aisle. Over and over again throughout their lives, children who have suffered a loss will be reminded of it, saddened by it, and affected by it in new ways. This grief is never as intense as the early grief, but it is grief nonetheless, and it must be honored and respected by us as parents.

Gregory Floyd says that as each year goes by the horrible images of his son lying unconscious on the front lawn become more muted, and the images of John Paul happy and laughing become more vibrant. However, he fully expects his children to "revisit" their grief at different moments in their lives.

"While life moves on and is full of the good things, we will have moments of this reality piercing our awareness as well as our hearts until the day we die," he says "I have no doubt about that whatsoever. It doesn't mean that life isn't happy. It means that it's happy, plus there will be piercing moments."

My own grief over my mother's death resurfaced when I had my children. It was most dramatic when Noah was born, since he was my first, and I had so many questions that could not be answered. I wanted my mother to be there to tell me about her experiences as a new mother. I was angry over what seemed like an unjust situation. My child was missing a grandparent, and I could never convey to him what she was truly like. When Olivia came along three and a half years later, I grieved again but in a different way. I was more melancholy. The acceptance came more readily, and that made everything that much sadder. How was it possible that I had gotten used to the absence of my mother? Even as an adult, that realization can take you aback.

Those feelings can be even stronger for a child who lost a parent before he had any conscious memories of their time together. When he regrieves later in life, there are no happy images to conjure up, no words of wisdom to fill the clanging void. For these children, it is especially important for surviving parents, siblings, grandparents, and extended family and friends to do all that they can to forge a connection to the deceased parent.

If a child is only three years old when her mother dies, then it is up to the survivors to make that parent a kind of presence in the child's future. Through pictures, stories, and memorials, that child can have happy memories to fall back on as she grows and reflects on her mother's death in more mature ways.

As I recalled at the beginning of this book, I was only five years old when my grandfather died. I talked about him pushing me in a swing hanging from his willow tree and about his relentless teasing. At this point, I don't know if those are real memories or memories that were created after years and years of hearing those happy stories. For me it doesn't really matter. They are part of my conciousness and help me to remember my grandfather fondly.

I have done something similar with my son. Because he will never know his grandmother, I make it a point to tell him stories, show him pictures, and recall the many happy times I shared with my mother. As a result, he will sometimes say, "I wish I could meet her." While in one sense that is a sad-sounding statement, for me it is a very positive sign. It means that I am passing on enough of my mother to make my child miss her, in a sense, even though he never knew her.

Are we open or closed to our children?

Sometimes our children amaze us with their perceptiveness, their understanding, and their ability to withstand adult-sized emotions despite their child-sized frames. Parents who allow their children to be themselves, who are willing to listen to their expressions of sadness and look for signs of sorrow, are often surprised by their children's strength.

Kathy Duke says that because of her son's experiences with his sister Emma's death and the death of other friends at the Ronald McDonald House where they stayed during Emma's illness, he understands that sometimes children die. "By the time Joseph was six years old he had a tremendous amount of loss. I have to give a lot of credit to him. He has always been really good at articulating his feelings, and he has not suppressed them," she says.

Although Kathy doesn't want to take any credit for Joe's healthy journey through grief, she should. She talks with Joe about Emma whenever they see something that reminds them of her. Two years after her death, they still hang Emma's stocking up at Christmas. They manage to remember Emma without getting pulled down by their grief.

"She's just still a part of us. I think that helps Joe—it certainly helps us—because we don't want to act like it never happened. I have had a lot of people tell me that they are amazed at how open and how articulate Joe is about his feelings. One time he came home from kindergarten just months after Emma died with a picture that had a rainbow at the top. It was supposed to be whatever you wish for, and it said, 'I wish my sister could come back.'"

Joe is lucky because his mother was willing to let him say what needed to be said and to remember his sister at Christmas or any other time her memory popped into his head. Other children are not always so fortunate. We parents and other adults sometimes hide our emotions and, without realizing it, make our children think that they shouldn't express their feelings either.

Often children will take the lead in discussing their emotions when the adults around them will not. The Dougy Center in Portland, Oregon, was established in response to a young boy's desperate attempt to find someone willing to talk to him about his impending death. His name, of course, was Dougy, and he had an inoperable brain tumor. He wrote a letter to death-and-dying expert Elisabeth Kübler Ross asking why adults wouldn't talk to him about the fact that he knew he was dying. She wrote and sent back to him a little booklet that is now called "A Letter to a Child with Cancer" or "The Dougy Letter." Dougy took it around to the other kids at the hospital and decided that if the adults wouldn't talk to them, they'd talk to each other. A nurse at the hospital was so impressed by how Dougy got the other children to open up that she decided to start a program to help kids dealing with terminal illness or the death of someone they love. That program grew into the Dougy Center.

Donna Schuurman, executive director of the Dougy Center, says that most problems stem from our fear of death and our fear of not knowing what to say to our children. Often we can't deal with our children's pain or don't think it's healthy to dwell on the matter, so we pressure our children to "get over" their grief quickly. "There are some parallels to sex education," Schuurman says. "Often what happens is nothing. People think kids will figure it out. We make it into a big deal, and it wouldn't have to be if it were incorporated naturally and not avoided."

What do we say?

It's almost never easy to know exactly what to say when a child is in crisis. We usually feel our way along. Too often I slip into a preachy mode when I'm talking to Noah about something serious, or I digress and lose him, and my point, along the way. When it comes to helping our grieving children, less is more.

Peter Assumma, funeral director of Assumma-Shankey Funeral Home in Pearl River, New York, says that if we could look at life and death as a child does, we would find the subject very simplistic and very real.

"Most of the questions children have are very basic. Parents get flustered by it because they are not listening to the questions," he says.

Say a child's grandmother dies, and that grandmother always made the child soup. Upon hearing of his beloved grandma's death, the child's only comment may be, "Who is going to make me soup now?" The parents, reeling from their own grief and unable to understand how their child could be thinking about soup, begin to talk about death and angels and heaven.

"The kid wants to know who's making the soup," explains Assumma. "He wants to know who's going to feed him and clothe him."

It helps if we can hold our tongue and let our children speak their minds, being careful to convey to them through our body language, eye contact, and tone that we are interested in and open to what they are saying. Turn toward them, speak in a normal tone and at a normal speed, and let your face reflect your empathy and concern. Sometimes when I'm talking to Noah, I get a very serious look. He usually lets me know by saying, "Why do you have that face on, Mom?" It immediately brings me out of whatever it is that's troubling me and reminds me to lighten up. Kids notice things like that, so we need to be aware of them as well.

We also don't want to get to a point where we're finishing our children's thoughts, interrupting them, or telling them what they're feeling. We have to give them whatever time they need to tell us in their own way what's happening. When that's done, then we can restate what they've said to let them know that we heard and understood them. For example, "It sounds as though you're really angry about Grandpa's death. Is that right?"

We can also phrase our questions in ways that will encourage our children to open up rather than simply reply with a yes or no answer. "Do you want to join a grief support group to help you deal with your anger?" will not do as much for a child as "Do you think there is anything we can do to help you deal with this anger?" The first question forces the child into a decision. The second question allows him to talk about his feelings and maybe come up with a solution of his own, which will be empowering in and of itself.

Sometimes our kids will say nothing at all. That's probably when we're most likely to start talking and asking

LEARNING TO LISTEN

ALLOW YOUR CHILDREN TO EXPRESS ANY AND ALL EMOTIONS, as long as those expressions do not hurt them or anyone else. Expect some pretty strong reactions from children who are experiencing the loss of a family member. Anger, sadness, denial, fear, withdrawal—all of these reactions come with the territory. Don't give in to your urge to put a lid on it. Allow your child the freedom to go where she needs to go emotionally. That being said, don't allow your child to spiral downward into a dangerous emotional hole where rage or depression or fantasy become the new reality. Provide ample room for your child's emotions but be ready to step in with the safety net of your parenting experience and love when those emotions get too big for him or her to handle.

a lot of questions. There's that need to fill the void. We want to get to the bottom of the problem, to do our duty as parents. Sometimes that means doing nothing. If our children are not ready to talk, our pushing and prodding will probably only make things worse. That doesn't mean that we should ignore or abandon them. It does mean that we should find a way to coexist with the silence. Suggest an outing to a park or try cooking a favorite meal together. Working together—even in silence—may be enough to make your child relax and open up.

VALIDATE FEELINGS BY ACKNOWLEDGING THAT THEY ARE NORMAL. Sometimes kids need only to hear that their fear, anger, sadness, confusion, or guilt is normal. Let them witness some of your own emotions. Don't pretend that you are not angry or sad just to protect your children. Simply telling your children that it's OK to feel sad or scared or mad is often enough to let them release their feelings.

EXPECT YOUR CHILDREN TO APPROACH GRIEF IN DIFFERENT WAYS. No two children will experience a death the same way. Some will want to talk about their deceased loved one; others will retreat to a place of silence for a while. Every child is

(continued)

unique, as is every family. How your children respond to a loss will depend on how they respond to things in general and how your family handles crises of any kind. Does everyone work themselves up into a frenzy? Do you hold a family meeting to talk and pray? Do the parents pit themselves against one another? Do the children get cut out of meaningful discussions? All of these things will influence how children grieve. Try to keep them in the loop. Don't allow anger or sadness to separate you from your children. Use the strength of your family to get through this difficult time together.

EXPECT YOUR CHILDREN TO "REGRIEVE" THROUGHOUT THEIR LIVES. Any significant loss your children experience will be with them forever—at least in some ways. Although the initial mind-numbing grief will pass with time, a less virulent form of grief will probably remain for years and years. Be prepared for it as major milestones approach— anniversaries, birthdays, favorite holidays, graduations, marriages, births, illnesses, and deaths. It is not unusual for children to experience milder forms of grief at any or all of these occasions.

Replacing the Bad Memories

ACTIVITY

Pastoral counselor Dorothy Armstrong says that we parents can help our children move through their grief by helping them "reframe" the pictures that may flash through their minds. Perhaps the only image a child has of his deceased father is that of him on his deathbed, or at his wake. That image can keep a child trapped emotionally in one place for a long time. We don't want our children to forget things that happened, but we do want them to replace the continuous loop of negative images with more positive ones.

"Children are so good at this," says Armstrong, who is also trained in neuro-linguistic programming. "You want to help your child in grief to reframe a memory so that same painful picture doesn't keep playing over and over."

STEP 1. Ask your child to think about the memory or picture that comes to mind whenever he thinks of his deceased loved one. Is it happy, sad, frightening? Is that image keeping him from doing other things?

STEP 2. Now start talking to your child about the happiest memory he has of his loved one. Is it a special vacation they took together, nightly bedtime stories they read, trips to the library they took each week, warm hugs they shared before heading out to school and work each day?

STEP 3. Tell your child to try to turn off the sad "tape" that has been playing in his mind. Put this new, happy memory in its place and let it be the image that

(continued)

ACTIVITY

appears instead. By changing the way a child pictures a scene, we can change his emotions and even a bit of his history.

STEP 4. Recognize that it may take time for your child to reach a point where he is able to do this. It is only normal for him to focus on his sorrowful memories for a certain amount of time. Eventually it will become easier to push the sad memories out of the way to make room for happier thoughts.

Ways to Encourage Reframing

ACTIVITY

WATCH VIDEOS AND LOOK THROUGH PHOTO ALBUMS. Let your child see his loved one laughing and enjoying himself. Talk about those times and try to recapture some of the happiness.

WORK IN YOUR LOVED ONE'S GARDEN, bake her favorite cookie recipe, listen to her favorite CD, rent her favorite movie. Find a way to recall the joy she found in simple things, and see if your child can grab some of that joy for himself.

TRY TO IMAGINE A DIFFERENT ENDING to your loved one's life. Picture her getting married, having children, growing old, doing the things she loved. Allow your child to use his imagination to create happy scenes. This doesn't mean we should encourage our children to live in a fantasy world but instead to see their loved ones in ways that bring them peace.

8

Spiritual Support: Managing the Role of Faith in Grieving

- **Do our children have faith?**

- **Where was God?**

- **What is heaven?**

- **How do we help a teenager's grief?**

- **What is the role of ritual and community?**

"I am the resurrection and the life; whoever believes in me, even if he dies, will live."
John 11:25

Andrew kept saying, "It's all my fault, Mommy." We just explained to him that God is in control of our lives and that it was Peter's time. I don't think we could have gotten through it without faith. We told Andrew that Peter is in heaven. How he got to heaven I'm not sure he ever really understood. I think he thought his whole body went to heaven. When we visited the cemetery, we would say that his body is underneath here and his soul is in heaven.

One day when we were staying at a cabin in the woods, we were eating donuts. Andrew said, "I bet you Rock is in heaven having donuts right now with Jesus and Mary. I bet he's having the chocolate one." He just thinks that he is up there playing and having a good time, that he never gets hurt.

—Carol Hyrcza, whose three-and-a-half-year-old son,
Peter, drowned on a family outing

✑

Faith may not get us through our grief any faster, but it certainly can make the journey a lot less harrowing. If we have passed on to our children our belief in resurrection and eternal life, they, too, will have something to turn to in their sorrow. That doesn't mean that they won't question God's wisdom, or even accuse God of taking revenge on them by stealing away a loved one. All of those reactions are normal. In fact, we parents go through many of the same emotions. But in the end, faith offers a kind of support that cannot be found anywhere else.

Father Terence Curley, president of the National Catholic Bereavement Ministry and author of several books on loss and grief, says that faith during grief is crucial. "I don't think faith is something added on; it is essential for the grieving process. It's the way in which we bring some meaning out of all the chaos. Faith and trust are synonymous, and you can almost use the two words interchangeably with a child."

It's best if we parents reflect on our own beliefs before we utter a word to our children. Do we feel confident telling our children that their grandma is with God? Do we really believe that death is just another part of life? Do we believe that our deceased loved one is still watching over us and that we will see her again? Once we come to terms with those questions, we can talk to our children about trust, about love, about hope, and about the belief that one day we will be reunited with our loved ones in heaven.

"Hopefully, the role of religion is to tie the whole thing together," says Father Curley. "As a vehicle for children, it is an essential one because in our faith we want to teach them early on that life isn't taken away; life is changed. The whole idea is that, as with an adult, you take the loss that a child has and place it into the context of faith, or into the context of trust, and that we trust in God. To do anything else would be to do a disservice to the whole experience of life for the child."

Do our children have faith?

From early infancy, a child's faith is forming. The baby who feels secure with his parents and trusts that they will keep him from harm begins to sense the love of a more powerful being. As a child grows and becomes more aware of the world around him, he realizes that his parents are separate from himself and that God is totally other. At about this time, children begin to use their imaginations to form pictures of God. Before long, they weave together what they have been taught, what they have overheard, and what they have imagined.

Michael Brown, a chaplain and clinical pastoral education coordinator for Franciscan Skemp Healthcare, Inc., in La Crosse, Wisconsin, says that the best time to talk to children about death and resurrection is before the crisis hits. "Ask what they think happens when you die. Where do they think they came from? What do they think heaven is like? Where is

God? Get them to tell you what they think, because in a way they already have some knowledge."

It helps if we can get past our own fears about death and talk honestly to our children about our faith. "It's a matter of accepting death as a normal part of life. Children shouldn't be shielded from that," says Brown.

Think about the last time you grieved for someone or something that disappeared from your life. There was probably a pain at the very center of your being, the feeling that the heartache would never subside.

When I lost a baby through miscarriage, I sat down in the shower one day and cried at the top of my lungs while the water poured over my head. I cried because of my sadness, I cried out in anger with God, I cried for the baby I would never know. At the time I thought I would never feel whole again. Grief can be like that. It can leave us aching inside.

Children are no different. No one can take those feelings of sorrow away from a grieving child, and no one should try. In some ways, we each have a right to grieve, to mourn, to let the sadness overwhelm us to a point.

Dorothy Armstrong, a New Jersey–based pastoral counselor who works with people in grief, says that most people do not want to be denied their time in grief. "To miss someone whom I loved—that has a divine flavor. Jesus loved Lazarus and groaned at his tomb because he wanted him alive. That pain in one's heart—that is not a bad thing, as long as it's life-giving," she says. "When you love people and you miss them, that is a very beautiful pain. It reaches a point in our innermost beings, in the depths of our faith. That's a pain that I don't want to be totally deprived of, the pain of love."

Children have a natural affinity for spirituality that is strengthened by the beliefs that have been incorporated into their lives, Armstrong says. "We have this very dynamic faith. Even children can talk about heaven, and they grasp it so easily."

Where was God?

For adults and children alike, feeling abandoned by God can be the ultimate feeling of loneliness. We look to God for protection, for the answers to our prayers. When something devastating happens, we wonder how God could allow—or even cause—this tragedy. It can shake our faith, and it can leave us feeling as though we have to go through this difficult journey alone.

Jennifer Morgan says that she questioned her faith in the wake of her fourteen-year-old brother's death. "We went to church as a family every weekend, and we were sent to Catholic schools. How could God do this to us?" she says. "At my Catholic high school, God was at the core of our school. I secretly hated God for what He did. Later when I left for college, I chose not to attend church—not until my senior year. One of the classes I chose for my psychology minor was on death and dying. I not only found myself learning about the subject but also growing spiritually."

Jennifer's mother, Lorraine Wilson, remembers her own faith crisis after Robby's death, saying that she continued to take the children to Mass on Sunday despite her own doubts and anger.

"In the beginning faith was very important. It got me through," says Lorraine. "Then, as reality set in, you realize that you lost a child and he's not coming back. You get very angry with God. We still went to church because of the children.

"Sometimes I would just sit in church and look at Jesus on the cross and think about the fact that Mary went through this. She lost her son, and I am certainly no better than her. I got angry with God, but then my faith returned. I am a firm believer that I am going to be reunited with Robby."

Witnessing a strong belief in God—especially in times of crisis or sorrow—can serve grieving children well. They learn that even in the midst of doubt and anger and sadness, they can talk to God. They learn that it is normal to question their faith and that, when all is said and done, they can rely on and return to their beliefs.

As a cemetery director, Regis Flaherty has seen the power of faith firsthand in his dealings with grieving families over the past twenty-six years. He has often been privy to their innermost emotions and beliefs. What he has seen has convinced him that faith provides comfort to adults and children alike.

"Parents have to try to give children a concept of resurrection, that life is not being ended but changed. It's important for parents to understand those faith issues and have a way to communicate them," he says. "Try to convey to the child your belief that we continue to help those who have died through prayer, that we believe they are with Jesus, and that in the resurrection we will be reunited to them again."

Praying for the dead can be a blessing. All these years later, I remember saying my bedtime prayers and including "Grandpa in heaven." Now my own children say the same bedtime prayers and include their "Grandma in heaven." It helps keep her memory alive. It helps to know that we can still connect to her in some way.

We can teach our children to remember loved ones and friends not only at bedtime but during Mass or on special feast days, holy days, or anniversaries. We can simply mention their names or we can say more formal prayers. Either way the power of prayer cannot be overestimated.

What is heaven?

Thinking that children are too young to understand spiritual issues is nothing new. After all, Jesus had to admonish his followers, saying, "Let the children come to me." We parents often think like those early disciples. Maybe it's because we are dealing with our own faith issues, or maybe we just don't realize how deeply our children have been touched by the spiritual lessons they have been taught.

Gregory Floyd witnessed his own children's deep spirituality both before and after their brother's death. "You can talk to children about heaven and about the deep realities of life," he says. "We radically underestimate the spirituality of children. They latch onto things, not with the depth of an adult, but sometimes in their very simplicity they transcend some of the things that the adults are struggling with."

Noah recently asked me about heaven. Even now, after months and months of research and writing on this topic, I still cringe a bit when I start to explain things. Will I pick the right words and the right images? We talked about heaven and how it is the place we will go after we die, the place where we will be with God and with people who have already died. We talked about the fact that it's not anything we can see or anything we can really know because no one on earth has ever seen it.

"Is heaven in outer space?" Noah asked, looking up at the planets and stars suspended from his bedroom ceiling. We talked a little more about how heaven is beyond outer space, beyond anything we can imagine. I am absolutely sure that he'll ask me these very same questions again, and I'll answer them again. Eventually we'll come up with an answer that satisfies us both.

Older children may want to talk about purgatory. The Catechism of the Catholic Church says that this is a place where "all who die in God's grace and friendship" will go if they need further purification to get into heaven. That's a nice, succinct explanation, one that should suffice. It is not hell. It is not punishment—that much can be made clear to any child old enough to ask about purgatory or to learn about it in religion class.

Chaplain Michael Brown says that the key to discussing faith issues with children is to not expect children to be at a stage that is above where they are developmentally. "It doesn't really do any good to start quoting Scripture or start trying to teach doctrine to a four-year-old. That's not the way they understand the world. You need to talk to children about faith and get them to tell you the stories they weave together."

So how do we tell a young child what happens to us after we die? We can simply explain what we believe—that our soul continues to live, that we will see our loved one again in heaven, that God promised us a place in heaven with him for all time. If a child is old enough to know more about the life of Jesus, we can rely on more explicit stories from Scripture about how Jesus taught us that there would be no more death.

If our children are too young to grasp the idea that a person's body is no longer thinking or feeling, we can offer a more concrete example of why the body is not needed after death.

"Compare it to something in a box," says Brown. "When you take the things out, you no longer need the box. That's not exactly theologically correct, but we're not dealing with cognitive stuff. You just want to help children understand that this person isn't suffering. They're not feeling sad. They don't feel cold. They're not asleep. Their body isn't working at all, and they don't need that body. God has given them a new one. We will see them again in that new body when we have died and we have received our new bodies."

How do we help a teenager's grief?

Because teens are desperately trying to develop their own individuality, talking to them about faith in the midst of grief can be a lesson in futility. They often reject whatever their parents say, and lessons in faith are no exception. Although we parents should continue to set limits, it's best to do so knowing that our children must go through this phase in order to emerge as healthy, independent adults.

Michael Brown says that what's most important to a teen at this point in her faith and grief is not what we say but what we do. "Kids at this age are very much into faith in action," he says. "They're also going to be very justice-minded about it when somebody close to them dies. They're going to say, 'Look, you always told me God is a loving God. Why did God take this person?' You're not going to be able to answer that question simply, and it's kind of futile to try because he's got a point. You've got to be able to say, 'I don't know.'"

Teens are likely to feel very angry about death and will be thrown off by the fact that the crisis will challenge whatever image they may still have of a warm and loving God. "It's going to shake that to its roots, and it's not going to be resolved in one conversation," says Brown.

Teens will watch to see how the adults around them are working through their own questions about death and faith. What we as parents can do is give them our example, be willing to talk about difficult issues, and let them have their opinions.

What is the role of ritual and community?

Perhaps there is nothing so comforting during a time of grief than the rituals of our faith and our cultures. From the wake to the burial, religious services are intended to be a healing balm, not a burden. It is a way for us to remember our loved one and to say one last good-bye. Too often, however, children are left out of the equation. (In chapter 9, we will take an in-depth look at the rituals surrounding death.)

Cemetery director Regis Flaherty says that the prayers we recite at the wake, the funeral Mass, and the cemetery are important for our transition from accepting the death of our loved one to adjusting to life without that person. "To think it's any less important to a child is naïve," he says. "Obviously their understanding level is different, so the way we communicate things to them needs to be at their level. But they need to have the same kind of process occur for them."

For Catholics, the Order of Christian Funerals, which was revised and reissued in 1989, calls on all parishioners to minister to bereaved persons of all ages. The order no longer emphasizes only the mechanics of the event but the heart of the matter, which is that people in grief need other people to help them through it. Those other people often can be found sitting in the pews around you on a Sunday morning.

Father Terence Curley, who talks about the new order in his books on Catholic funerals and ministry to the bereaved, says that the role of the parish is to be the loving listener. "We have wonderful people in parishes, wonderful resources, like eucharistic ministers, lectors, people who work in the field of bereavement and some who don't. Usually people who are willing to be present and loving listeners have an awareness of the process to a degree, far better than any other professional approach, because grief is not an illness. It's one of the passages we have to go through," Father Curley says. "Churches and temples are in a position to offer something that is so very powerful."

If a parish doesn't offer programs specifically for children in grief, ask your pastor for a referral to another local group or program. The parish can provide much more than ongoing prayerful support. It can link us to the people and programs that will help us. Our parish can serve as a bridge of faith for us and our children as we journey from grief to healing.

A DISCUSSION ON FAITH

It's hard to know what to say to our kids when they ask tough questions about God and death. Since I'm often at a loss for the right answers, I asked a priest friend of mine, Msgr. William Benwell, to give us parents a little guidance in this department. Msgr. Benwell, who has been pastor of Our Lady of the Mount Parish in Warren, New Jersey, for more than twelve years, provides some general suggestions as well as specific answers:

SOME GENERAL TIPS FOR PARENTS, TEACHERS, AND OTHER ADULTS

NURTURE YOUR CHILD'S FAITH *NOW* by making expressions of faith an integral dimension of your family's life. Attend church regularly as a family. Pray together and read stories of faith. Share how *you* have experienced God's love and presence. If you do these things, your child will already have embraced many of the answers to the "faith" questions that come up when someone she loves dies.

DON'T PASS UP THE CHANCE TO MINISTER TO A GRIEVING CHILD because you don't have "the answer" to that child's grief. There are no words that can take away the hurt, confusion, and fear that death brings up, but never underestimate how comforting your interest and your presence can be.

(continued)

ANSWERING SOME OF THE TOUGH QUESTIONS

Q: Are suffering and death God's way of punishing us for being bad?

A: Jesus was asked this question several times and always his answer was no. (Luke 13:1–5; John 9:2–3). Jesus revealed that God is understanding, forgiving, merciful; the Bible tells us that "God is love" (1 John 4:8). One who loves does not seek to hurt others.

Q: If God loves us, why does he allow people to die?

A: Would you say a friend was kind and loving if he planned every minute of your time together, never letting you have a say in choosing when and where and what you should play? Because God *is* loving, God has given human beings the freedom to choose how we will live our lives, as well as to create the kind of world in which to live them. A long, long time ago, our ancestors in faith chose to reject God's original plan for us, and so we must live with our human shortcomings, such as the fact that our bodies are not indestructible.

God's love for us is always greater than any of our faults or imperfections, and so God has placed in every human being a soul (the thinking, feeling part of us), which will never die. While we certainly are sad when we can no longer enjoy our earthly life with the people we love, we also know that God has prepared for their souls a greater, permanent place with him in heaven.

Q: Where is heaven and what is it like?

A: Heaven isn't a place we can see or visit; it is a bit of a mystery, something we can't fully explain or understand. But we know heaven exists because Jesus talked about it many times (e.g., Matthew 28:18; Mark 10:21; John 14:2–3). We also know it is a wonderful place because in heaven there is no pain or suffering. In heaven we'll see God as he really is; we'll live with God, and all who are friends of God, forever. Whatever heaven is like exactly, we won't be disappointed.

Q: When people die, do they become angels?

A: Angels and human beings are two different creations of God. The Bible tells us that right now we are a "little less than the angels," (Psalms 8:6) who are always with God in heaven. A person in heaven will be made to be *like* an angel—perfect and perfectly happy.

ACTIVITY

A Time and Place for Prayer

When we think about prayer, we don't have to limit our images to kneeling in a pew at church. Your prayer could be a long walk with your child in the crisp evening air. Watch the moon rising, breathe deeply of God's goodness, look at the stars, talk about things you see along the way. Anything and everything we do can become a prayer. In fact, our lives would be so much happier if we could all approach every day that way. When we are in grief, prayer is even more important. Here are some suggestions for bringing God into your home and your life.

BEGIN BY SIMPLY MAKING ROOM FOR GOD—in your consciousness, in your schedule, in your home. That doesn't mean that you have to carry around a prayer book or that every prayer has to be related to your deceased loved one. It means learning to find God in the ordinary events of the day—in line at the drive-in window at the bank, walking your child across the parking lot before school, in the silence before a roaring fire.

SET ASIDE REGULAR TIMES TO PRAY, times that your child will come to expect and anticipate—in the morning, before dinner, at bedtime. You can rely on favorite prayers that you remember from your childhood or experiment with creating prayers of your own.

TEACH YOUR CHILD TO TALK TO GOD. Don't simply recite a laundry list of wishes, but rather learn to express your sorrows, your joys, your fears. Children will begin to see God as a friend, someone who will listen to her troubles when she is lying awake at night.

CREATE A SPECIAL PLACE TO PRAY—around a small table in the living room, kneeling next to your child's bed, hands joined around the kitchen table. Add candles, a statue or cross, flowers, an inspiring quote for reflection, and perhaps a photo of your loved one or some other remembrance. Silence the television, radio, stereo, and telephone during times of prayer.

GO TO CHURCH and let your child light a candle in your loved one's memory. Kneel down together in prayer.

ARRANGE TO HAVE MASS OFFERED IN YOUR LOVED ONE'S NAME. Attend with your child, and then do something together afterward.

ACTIVITY

9

Ways to Remember: Ritual and the Creation of Memories

- **How young is too young?**

- **How do we prepare our children before they attend a wake or funeral?**

- **How can we make the funeral service a meaningful experience for our children?**

- **How will attending the burial or cremation service affect the grieving process?**

Rituals remind us that life is eternal.

Rev. Terence P. Curley, *Six Steps for Managing Loss*

Pink crepe myrtle blossoms hang overhead as dozens of people gather on the shores of the Colorado River. A little boy in a burnt orange Texas Longhorns T-shirt clutches a bouquet of pink and yellow gerbera daisies with a profound sense of seriousness. A teenage boy in baggy jeans nonchalantly twirls a solemn long-stem rose between his thin fingertips. A young girl in a frilly, cream-colored lace dress kneels down in the parched grass to touch a name on a stone marker.

Under a cloudless blue October sky, the children and their families look at a map to find "their" trees, marked with heart-shaped name tags along the river that is known as Town Lake in downtown Austin, Texas. They are searching for the trees they have donated in memory of deceased parents and grandparents, brothers and sisters, friends and relatives. They are searching for a way to bring some closure and some peace to their lives after the devastation of death and grief.

While the adults shake hands, wipe away tears, and offer hugs to one another, the children find their own ways to cope. They watch the birds flying overhead, find a thick tree limb to climb, follow the path of a cyclist on the nearby hike-and-bike trail, twirl a white rose like a weightless baton. This ceremony is as much for them as it is for the adults, and they trail their families up to the podium to accept certificates and hear the names of the deceased read out in a roll call that is at once full of sorrow and full of hope.

A young girl armed with a disposable camera points and clicks, capturing for posterity—and perhaps for comfort on the long road to healing—a mother's name carved in stone, a fragile sapling blowing in the autumn breeze, a celebration that insists that death will not have the last word.

❧

If you take ritual and ceremony out of life, you take away so much of the stuff that gives us our memories and allows us to hold onto events that might otherwise fade from our mind's eye. From the baptism that celebrates new life to the anointing of the sick that signals preparation for death, our lives move to the rhythm of rituals that not only impart meaning but also leave indelible marks on our hearts.

Remember the way your first communion dress puffed out when you sat down in the pew, the way your high-school ring caught the sunlight as you accepted your diploma, the way the church smelled of gardenias when you walked down the aisle to get married? The major milestones of our lives serve as the bookmarks that allow us to turn back to earlier chapters and relive a particular day, if only for a fleeting moment.

Death and grief and mourning require the same attention to ritual, especially for children who often have no other way to cope with the loss of a beloved relative or friend. Most of us seek the closure and finality that come from attending a funeral or throwing dirt on a casket as it is lowered into the ground. Adults often think that children do not want or need such stark reminders of their loss, but the truth is that they do need the opportunity to participate in ceremonies or create rituals of their own. It is a way for them to bookmark the life and death of their deceased loved one so that it can be looked up, relived, mourned, or celebrated whenever there is a longing or a need.

How young is too young?

Mention the subject of children and funerals, and inevitably the first question to come up is whether children can be too young to attend a wake, funeral, burial, or even a memorial service. As adults who have weathered and, in many cases, assimilated the death-denying precepts of our society, it is only logical that we project our views and feelings onto the children in our lives. We assume that the sight of Grandma lying in a casket draped with flowers cannot possibly be healthy for someone so young.

The reality, however, is that young children are often more adept at handling the difficult aspects of death than many adults. Seeing the peaceful smile on Grandma's face, saying good-bye one last time, dropping a note or a favorite trinket into the casket as one last reminder of the happy times that were shared are ways for children to reconcile Grandma's absence from the dinner table with the abstract explanation of death that Mom and Dad gave them before walking into the funeral home.

Funeral director Peter Assumma says that parents should bring their children to a funeral home for an informal visit in much the same way they might take them to the fire station or the library. "If we expose our children to death, that's the only way they are going to have a full understanding of life. When folks talk about bringing kids in, I tell them that I can guarantee that they won't have a problem. I tell them that if the kids are crying, it is usually because they are picking up on the adults' moods."

Assumma, who has worked in the funeral industry for more than twenty years, turned the smoking lounge in his funeral home into a playroom for children so that they can watch videos, play games, make noise, and let off steam when sitting still in the viewing room upstairs gets to be too much for them.

It is not always easy, however, to convince us parents that our children may benefit from attending a wake or funeral. Often we are so caught up in our own sorrow over the loss that we forget that our children have to accept and process the death as well. With or without our encouragement, children will find ways to cope with death, but it is the job of parents and other responsible adults to help them cope in the healthiest ways possible.

Assumma tells parents to bring children to the funeral home before the public viewing so that he can talk to them, answer questions, and allow them to view their loved one in private. Most questions that children have at viewing are far more basic than any theological discussions of what happens to us when we die. They want to know how Grandpa feels lying in the casket—if he can hear, if he can hurt, if he's going to wake up. Assumma says that since caskets with only the top half open are often the norm, many children fear that the deceased person's legs have been chopped off. He makes a point of lifting the bottom half of the casket lid so that children can see the whole body, and even touch the legs if they like.

I witnessed that curiosity firsthand when my four-year-old niece's great-grandmother died. My sister carefully explained what she would see when she got to the funeral home and let her know that she did not have to get close to the casket if she did not want to. Once at the funeral home, however, Kaci could not stay away from the casket. She kept finding reasons to walk past it, to peer over the edge. She went out of her way to get a closer look at her great-grandma.

At one point, she began asking my husband, Dennis, what happened to her great-grandmother's legs. Just as Assumma points out, that was the one aspect of this whole experience that just did not sit right with her.

"Most kids want to touch the person. They are not afraid. They are so at ease with it," Assumma says. "I have never had a problem with a child."

That said, he estimates that only 50 to 60 percent of families allow children to attend the wake and funeral services he directs—something he attributes to a culture that has tried to remove the reality of death from public view. It was not all that long ago that people died at home and were even waked at home. Children and adults were more at ease with the idea of death because it was much more a part of normal life. Children saw grandparents, parents, even siblings, laid out in the living room as others kept vigil. Those days are gone, and with them has gone the healthy understanding that death is a sad but natural part of life.

Now we head to often-sterile funeral parlors where we can try to keep the image of death far from our homes and our daily lives. We attend services, send flowers, and offer prayers. But through it all we need to remember that wakes and funerals are much more than a polite way to honor the dead. They are a way to begin the grieving and the healing process—and that holds true for children as well as adults.

"There is genuinely a real need for us to see the physical remains. Our culture has gotten away from that," says Assumma. "Death has been one of the greatest taboos. The reality is that we all go through it. It's a natural process in the cycle of life, and we don't teach our children that."

Funeral and memorial services allow children to acknowledge that it's OK to die. They help them understand that there is a process that people go through in order to grieve and to celebrate the life of the person who has died. To help that process along, chaplains, priests, ministers, and funeral directors can provide workbooks that encourage children to express their feelings about death through drawings and other activities.

"Listen to your kids. Don't force them to go to the wake or funeral, but listen to them. If they want to go and if they want to participate, let them. Almost all kids want to. Give them the opportunity," says Assumma. "Our kids teach us brilliantly if we just watch them. Kids do know what's happening. It's so foolish to think they don't. The kids know that something is wrong, and you cannot exclude them from it."

How do we prepare our children before they attend a wake or funeral?

So, if we can't—or shouldn't—exclude our children from the funeral home and the cemetery, how do we go about including them in the healthiest ways? The first step is to offer our children the opportunity to attend the wake, funeral, or burial. Try to phrase the question in the most objective way possible so that you don't influence a decision one way or the other. Simply ask, "What do you think about going to the funeral with me?" If the answer is positive, the next step is to prepare the child for what she will see and hear.

The experience will vary greatly, depending on your child's age, your family's religious or ethnic customs, and the circumstances surrounding the death of the loved one. The best way to start a discussion on the subject is to begin with the basics: What is a funeral? What does the funeral home look like? What is a casket? What will be expected of the child once he or she is at the funeral home? What is cremation? What is a cemetery?

Toddlers, preschoolers, and other young children will want to know very simple details, like what color the flowers will be, or whether there will there be any snacks or juice. They need to know how things will look when they enter the funeral home, why there are so many chairs lined up in rows, why people are writing in a special book, why some people are laughing and some people are crying.

It's best to stick to simple and truthful answers. Talk about the casket, about why people send flowers. Ask if the child would like to send a flower arrangement in his name or if there is something else he would like to bring as a way of remembering Grandpa. Tell the child that he will have the chance to say a prayer near Grandpa, touch his hand, or simply sit in a chair nearby once he gets to the funeral home. Be sure to remind him that he doesn't have to do these things, but that he can do them if he wants.

The big questions that are likely to come from preschoolers and early elementary-school children will have to do with the physical appearance of the deceased person. Explain to them that Grandma isn't breathing anymore, that her body doesn't work, that she can't hear or talk or feel anything. Her heart has stopped beating. She is dead. It may sound harsh, but direct answers that don't fuel active imaginations are the best way to begin the acceptance process.

Of course, explaining all this won't necessarily ensure that your child won't come up with some pretty outrageous ideas of his own—or that some well-meaning adult won't put some ideas in his head.

When my three-year-old son attended the wake of an older woman we had known, I carefully went through all the proper explanations about her heart not beating and about how even though she looked like she was sleeping she was not. We answered every question he came up with at the funeral home and in the car. What I didn't know until later, however, was that the deceased woman's son kept telling Noah that she was "just sleeping." No sooner did we get in the car for the ride home when Noah looked at me and asked, "Why was that lady sleeping in the big toy box?" My husband and I tried quickly and simply to explain one more time that she was not asleep, and then we let the matter drop, hoping that this would not be the impression of death that would stick with him.

It's not a bad idea to let friends and relatives know what you have told your child about death and about your deceased loved one. Otherwise you, too, may find your careful preparations undone in a matter of seconds by someone who has different ideas about what children should and shouldn't know.

Older children, because they have more knowledge, also have more fears. They may worry about what will happen once the body goes into the ground, or imagine that the person is not really dead and will be closed in the casket alive. Once again, we can be direct, truthful, and sensitive. Explain that Grandma was examined by a doctor and prepared by the funeral home staff before she was put in the casket. Let them know that there is no doubt about her being dead. Explain that the casket is designed to protect the body once it is in the ground, but that Grandma's soul has already moved on to the next life. Although her body will be there under the stone marker for years to come, her spirit is alive for all time. She is with God.

We don't want to feed their fears or their imaginations, but we also need to make sure that we don't let them think that they have asked a foolish question. We can tell them the answers to their questions as best we can, and, if we don't know the answer, be honest and suggest that we talk to the funeral director, priest, or minister together.

Questions from teens are probably the most difficult to field. Some may be designed to shock us, others to see if we are as steadfast in our religious beliefs as we claim to be. Remember that teenagers are in the already difficult position of trying to separate from parents and siblings. A death, especially the death of a close family member or friend, will create friction as they strive to maintain their independence and seek support at the same time. They may act indifferent. They may say they don't want to attend the funeral at all. Simply offer them the opportunity, and explain that they will not get another chance to say this particular kind of good-bye.

How can we make the funeral service a meaningful experience for our children?

If you are a member of the immediate family, you can arrange to go to the funeral home early so that your child can ask

questions and view your loved one in private. If possible, talk
to the funeral director ahead of time so that he is aware of
your child's situation. Let him know if your child has ever
been to a funeral before, if she has any understanding of what
will happen at the funeral home, and if she has expressed
either an interest in or a fear of participating.

Once your child has been told what to expect, take
her by the hand and walk together to the casket. Kneel down
beside it, if your child seems open to that suggestion, and
talk about your loved one a bit before saying a prayer. Listen
for cues from your child. She may have questions or worries
that she wants to talk about, and it's OK to do that right
there in front of the body.

Don't try to hold back your own emotions either. Your
child will sense that something is wrong, if you are desperately
trying to keep from crying. Your child will learn from you that
it is OK to cry, that feeling sad is normal. When your child
sees that you are willing to let your feelings out, it opens the
door for her to do the same.

Remember to ask your child if she wants to bring a photo
or note or some other memento to leave behind in the casket.
That in itself can be a healing act that will make the child feel
forever connected in a physical way to the deceased loved one.

How will attending the burial or cremation service affect the grieving process?

The funeral Mass or service allows us parents ample opportunities to involve our children in concrete ways. Perhaps our

children can be altar servers or lectors. Maybe our family could bring up the gifts during the offertory procession or sing a special song as part of the service.

Father Terence Curley, who has written extensively about grief and loss, says that the more everyone takes part in things, the better off they are. "The good thing about looking at life and death is that we're on a journey, and that metaphor of journey is very, very important. It's never too early to teach a child that there's a journey, and the journey is toward the kingdom of heaven. Physically we're not here, but one day we'll be with God in a very special way."

Father Curley stresses that we parents should not feel we have to follow "a script," but should instead rely on our own instincts and our own deep and personal knowledge of our children.

"I think we write the script as we go along. It's like any other subject. It's almost like you have to find out what a child's perception is and let him tell you. And if there's any resistance along the way, well, act appropriately," he explains. "Maybe he's not quite ready to go into a viewing or to a wake or a vigil, although by and large I recommend it.

"So the rule of thumb is that you have to know where your child is, and I think the parent is the best of all educators. The bond of love is greatest between the parent and the child. We have to rely on that. The parent has to rely on that as well. You just make your best judgment at the time, as long as the child feels safe and feels secure."

That advice holds true for decisions on going to the crematory or attending the burial service as well. Some children may not be prepared for the idea of a cremation or the visual memory of seeing a casket lowered into the ground. Others will be comforted by the fact that they have seen for themselves. They won't have to rely on more frightening images of cremation, cemeteries, and graves.

Peter Assumma says that the best way to talk to children about cremation is to focus on the natural process, not so much on the details of how it is performed. "I would explain to them, in a sense, the story of *The Lion King,* the circle of life and how our body goes back to the earth. Cremation is just a much more rapid process than what we're used to," he says. "When I talk to folks, cremation is referred to as a 'radical' form of disposition—radical in the sense that the body is being brought to dust in a matter of hours as opposed to in a traditional burial when the body is being brought to dust over twenty years."

Even fire, he explains, can have a positive connotation if we look at it as a source of heat and not an element of destruction. "I would tend to go toward that positive side, not speaking about fire but about how cremation is accelerating the process of returning the body to dust."

That is also a good time to reiterate what we've already discussed—that a person who is dead cannot feel pain. When a loved one is cremated, we want to make sure our children understand that this process is not better or worse than traditional burial, just different. We can always turn to

Scripture and remind them of the words from Genesis 3:19 that we hear every Ash Wednesday: "For dust you are, and to dust you will return."(NIV)

Attending burial, too, can be very traumatic for children, but experts say that the image often helps children move through the grieving process more quickly. In fact, many people find cemeteries to be comforting, somewhere to connect in a physical sense with the deceased loved one. Walk through any cemetery and you're likely to see everything from flowers and vigil lights to balloons and stuffed animals decorating the headstones. It's not uncommon to see people talking to their deceased loved ones at a cemetery. On the other hand, some people—and this holds true for children as well as adults—don't find comfort or peace or any connection at the cemetery. To them it is a sad reminder of what they have lost, not a place to talk.

I have never found much meaning at the cemetery. It is the place where my mother's body is buried, but it is not the place where her spirit soars. I don't find a lot of comfort there. For my mother's sister, on the other hand, the cemetery is a place where she can be closer to my mother, where she can talk or remember happier times. It is a matter of personal taste, and as parents we should remember that our children may have the same strong feelings about cemeteries.

Ask your child what he thinks a cemetery is and what happens there. Let him ask questions and answer them as simply and directly as possible. Ask him if he wants to go to the burial or the cemetery at a later date to leave flowers or some other token. Be open to whatever answer you get.

"We go to the cemetery a lot," says Carol Hyrcza, whose three-year-old son, Peter, drowned during a family outing in 1996. Her older son, Andrew, who was particularly close to Peter, often asks to go the cemetery to visit his brother's grave.

"When he has a bad day or doesn't feel that good about what's going on at school or something, he'll say, 'I need to go to the cemetery.' He'll just stand there. Sometimes he'll cry, and he'll say, 'I feel better now.' It's a pain that Andrew will always have and I will always have. When Andrew cries, I just try to tell him that we're just so lucky that we had Peter for as long as we did, that he had such a wonderful relationship with his brother."

If we are willing to include our children in the rituals that are part of normal grief and mourning, we are likely to find that they are capable of handling so much more than we expect. Like Andrew Hyrcza, they may find comfort in the solitude of the cemetery. They may want to do all the things that we adults wish we could avoid. That's because children don't yet have all the fears and hang-ups that we adults have about death.

Noah has been asking me lately when we can go to the cemetery to see my mother's grave. Every time we drive past a cemetery, no matter where it is, he wants to know if that is where my mother is buried. I took him to my mother's grave when he was only five months old and again when he was three, the only times I was near enough to visit. We're making plans to go there again soon. What's most surprising is that the cemetery now holds more meaning to me than it ever did before. My children have given me that gift.

As Noah climbs on the headstone with a complete lack of fear or concern, I am awed by his acceptance of our reality, of his ability to grasp on some level that a woman he has never met, his grandmother, is buried there. He sees my tears and wants to make them go away, and in that instant I am once again keenly aware of everything I've learned during the course of writing this book. Children want to understand death. They need to grieve. They sense our sorrow, and they need us to sense theirs.

PREPARING FOR A WAKE

Going to a funeral home for the first time can be a frightening experience for kids of all ages. They don't know what to expect. They imagine all kinds of things. We can help ease the fears by preparing them for what they will see.

DESCRIBE THE PHYSICAL ATMOSPHERE OF THE FUNERAL HOME—what it looks like, if you expect a large crowd to be there, if there is a room designated for children who want to take a break from the viewing.

EXPLAIN WHAT TO EXPECT ONCE INSIDE THE VIEWING ROOM. There will be many chairs for those paying respects. There will be a kneeler beside the casket for those who want to say a prayer and a final good-bye. Discuss whether the casket will be open or closed (if you know this information). Call ahead and ask the funeral director if he is willing to talk to your children privately before the viewing.

LET YOUR CHILD KNOW THAT IT'S OK IF HE DOESN'T GO UP TO THE CASKET. On the other hand, also let him know that it's OK to lightly touch the person's hand or to leave a small memento in the casket as a farewell token.

(continued)

EXPLAIN THAT MOST PEOPLE WILL BE TALKING QUIETLY, but that others may be crying or laughing or talking loudly as they recall happy times they shared with the deceased loved one. Also explain that the immediate family (if you are not part of this group) will be greeting you in the viewing room. If you will be attending the wake on an evening when a clergy member will be leading prayers, explain this to your children so they are not confused or surprised.

TALK ABOUT WHY THE WAKE IS IMPORTANT. It is a way to say good-bye to a loved one, to celebrate her life, to honor her and to mourn her. If children don't want to attend, don't push them. Allow them to come to this gathering on their own terms or not at all.

SPECIAL TIPS FOR VERY YOUNG CHILDREN

It can be especially difficult to prepare toddlers or preschoolers for what they will see at a funeral home. Even with clear explanations, they will often be confused. Just try to use very simple and concise terms. These suggestions may work for older children as well, depending on the child and the situation.

- We're going to a funeral home, which is like a large house with many rooms.
- We'll see lots of people we know there. Some will want to talk to us. Aunt Sally may be crying since she is so sad that Uncle Paul died.
- Uncle Paul will be there in something called a casket, which is a special box used to bury people.
- He will look as though he's sleeping, but he's not. He's dead, which means he can't hear or feel anything. His heart is not beating. If you touch him, his skin will feel cold. He will look like the man you remember, but he will not act that way.
- People will walk up to the casket to say good-bye and to say a prayer. You can walk up with me if you like and we'll pray together. But, if you don't want to do that, you can sit in one of the chairs further back in the room.
- After we say a prayer, we'll talk to Aunt Sally to tell her how sorry we are that Uncle Paul died. Then we'll sit for a while and visit with friends and family. Everyone

(continued)

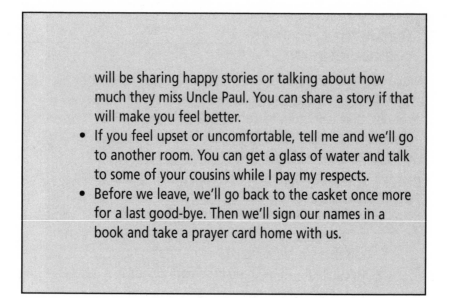

will be sharing happy stories or talking about how much they miss Uncle Paul. You can share a story if that will make you feel better.

- If you feel upset or uncomfortable, tell me and we'll go to another room. You can get a glass of water and talk to some of your cousins while I pay my respects.
- Before we leave, we'll go back to the casket once more for a last good-bye. Then we'll sign our names in a book and take a prayer card home with us.

Creating a Garden Memorial

STEP 1. Help your child find a special spot—your loved one's favorite spot in the yard, a spot with a beautiful view, or a shady, peaceful spot just right for reflection.

STEP 2. Clear a space for the memorial. The size of this space will depend on how elaborate you want the garden to be.

STEP 3. Let your child choose a plant (or two or three) that was a favorite of your loved one or something that reminds you of that person—yellow roses because yellow was her favorite color, a lilac bush like the one outside her house, a small Norwegian spruce to remind you of her homeland. Selections also will depend on the sun or shade available in the location, so be careful to choose wisely.

STEP 4. Once the plants are in the ground, create a marker of some sort. It could be as simple as a rock you and your child discovered on a walk or as elaborate as a professionally made statue. It's up to you, but try to choose something in keeping with your loved one's personality.

STEP 5. Make this spot a place where you and your child can come to reflect on your loved one's life, to cry when you are sad, and to laugh when you are happy. Water it, tend it, enjoy it.

ACTIVITY

ACTIVITY

Additional Ideas for Your Garden Site

ADD A PLACE FOR QUIET CONTEMPLATION—a large rock, a stone bench, or even a lawn chair. Your child may find that the spot becomes a favorite place to read, listen to music, or just observe nature.

ADD OTHER ELEMENTS to expand and beautify the site. A bird feeder or birdbath might be nice, if your loved one was fond of birds, or a statue of St. Francis of Assisi or the Blessed Mother, wind chimes, a pinwheel, a wind sock, a small pond or bubbling waterfall.

CREATE A PERSONALIZED MARKER for the site—a step-ping stone with your child's handprints or pretty seashells or rocks embedded in it, a rock with your loved one's name or simply the word *love* or *peace* painted on it. Kits are available in craft stores, but it's not difficult to make your own with cement and plastic tubs or child-friendly paint and a rock from your yard.

IF YOU DON'T HAVE SPACE OUTDOORS, consider doing a smaller version as a container garden. Buy an inexpensive clay pot and let your child decorate it with paint or glitter. After the decorating is complete, add a couple of plants, some col-ored stones, seashells, a small statue, or some other small remembrance. Put it in a special spot in your home—maybe the place where you gather for prayer or on a table near a sunny window.

Resources for Healing

Recommended Reading for Parents Who Are Helping a Child in Grief

A Grief Unveiled: One Father's Journey through the Death of a Child, by Gregory Floyd, Paraclete Press, 1999. A father's moving story of his journey through grief after the death of his six-year-old son.

Talking about Death: A Dialogue between Parent and Child, by Earl Grollman, Beacon Press, 1990. A classic that gives specific examples of how to talk to a child about death.

How to Go On Living When Someone You Love Dies, by Therese A. Rando, Bantam Books, 1991. Another classic that talks about death and grief in general, with a specific section on children and grief.

Six Steps for Managing Loss: A Catholic Guide through Grief, by Terence P. Curley, Alba House, 1997. A guidebook based on faith. Includes exercises for managing loss and a section on personal prayer.

Helping Children Cope with Grief, by Alan Wolfelt, Accelerated Development, Inc., 1983. An in-depth look at children and grief from the perspective of a psychologist who is considered a leader in the field.

Recommended Reading for Children Ages Four to Eight

Sad Isn't Bad: A Good-Grief Guidebook for Kids Dealing with Loss, by Michaelene Mundy, R.W. Alley (Illustrator), Abbey Press, 1998. A wonderful book by a mother, teacher, and school counselor. Helps children explore the many scary feelings and questions that death and grief bring up.

When a Pet Dies, by Fred Rogers, Putnam, 1988. A basic and helpful book by one of public television's most beloved figures.

Saying Goodbye to Daddy, by Judith Vigna, Albert Whitman & Co., 1991. A good book about a sad subject—a dad who dies in a car accident.

Lifetimes: A Beautiful Way to Explain Death to Children, by Bryan Mellonie and Robert Ingpen (Contributor), Bantam Books, 1983. This book uses the cycles of nature to talk about death. A good primer for those who want to bring up the subject ahead of time.

I'll Always Love You, by Hans Wilhelm, Crown, 1985. A wonderful book that focuses on life and love through the story of a dog's death.

What's Heaven? by Maria Shriver, Sandra Speidel (Illustrator), Golden Books, 1999. A mother and daughter talk about heaven following the death of a beloved great-grandmother.

The Fall of Freddie the Leaf, by Leo F. Buscaglia, Holt Rinehart Winston, 1982. The story of a leaf serves as a parable that sheds light on the mysteries of life and death.

The Saddest Time, by Norma Simon, Albert Whitman & Co., 1986. An emotional book that looks at the death of an uncle, the death of a boy who is hit by a car, and the death of a grandmother. Sections are split by verses.

Saying Good-Bye to Grandma, by Jane Resh Thomas, Marcia Sewall (Illustrator), Clarion Books, 1988. A longer story that focuses on funeral rituals as well as the loss of a grandparent.

Talking about Death? by Karen Bryant-Mole, Raintree Steck-Vaughn, 1999. A good primer for kids who are learning about death or dealing with their own reactions after the loss of a loved one.

When Dinosaurs Die: A Guide to Understanding Death, by Laurie Krasny Brown and Marc Tolon Brown (Illustrator), Little Brown & Company, 1996. Addresses children's fears about death.

Recommended Reading for Children Ages Nine to Twelve

The Kids' Book about Death and Dying: By and for kids, by Eric E. Rofes (Editor) and the Unit at Fayerweather Street School, Little Brown & Company, 1985. Young people talk about funeral customs, various types of loss, violent deaths, life after death.

When Someone Dies, by Sharon Greenlee, Bill Drath (Illustrator), Peachtree Publishers, 1992. A teacher and grief counselor explores a tough subject.

What on Earth Do You Do When Someone Dies? by Trevor Romain, Elizabeth Verdick, Free Spirit Press, 1999. Suggests ways of dealing with questions of loss that frequently come up.

Sky Memories, by Pat Brisson, Wendell Minor (Illustrator), Delacorte Press, 1999. A beautiful book about the death of a single mother written from her daughter's perspective.

Recommended Reading for Teens and Young Adults

The Grieving Teen: A Guide for Teenagers and Their Friends, by Helen Fitzgerald, Simon & Schuster, 2000. Renowned grief counselor focuses on the special needs of adolescents in grief.

Straight Talk about Death for Teenagers: How to Cope with Losing Someone You Love, by Earl A. Grollman, Beacon Press, 1993. Rabbi and grief expert uses prose-poem format to help teens coping with death of a family member or friend.

Recommended Reading for Parish Leaders, Funeral Directors, and Others Who Deal with Bereaved Children

The Ministry of Consolation: A Parish Guide for Comforting the Bereaved, by Terence P. Curley, Alba House, 1993. Chapter three focuses on "Grief through the Eyes of a Child."

Console One Another: A Guide for Christian Funerals, by Terence P. Curley, Sheed & Ward, 1993. Describes how a parish community can minister to bereaved members. Includes scriptural suggestions, prayers for special circumstances, and a section on how to discuss death with children.

Recommended Reading for Specialty Areas

A Piece of My Heart: Living through the Grief of Miscarriage, Stillbirth, or Infant Death, by Molly Fumia, Conari Press, 2000.

Breaking the Silence: A Guide to Help Children with Complicated Grief: Suicide, Homicide, AIDS, Violence, and Abuse, 2nd ed. by Linda Goldman, Brunner-Routledge, 2002.

Bart Speaks Out: Breaking the Silence on Suicide, by Linda Goldman, Western Psychological Services, 1998.

Recommended Videos for Parents and Other Adults

A Place Prepared: Helping Children Understand Death and Heaven, Paraclete Video Productions, 2000. A wonderful, forty-minute video to help parents and other adults talk with children about the inevitable losses they will encounter throughout their lives.

A Child's View of Grief, by Dr. Alan Wolfelt, Center for Loss and Life Transition. Twenty minutes.

A Teen's View of Grief, by Dr. Alan Wolfelt, Center for Loss and Life Transition. Forty minutes.

Organizations to Contact by Phone, Fax, Mail, or E-mail

The Compassionate Friends
P.O. Box 3696
Oak Brook, IL 60522-3696
Phone: 877/969-0010 (toll free)
Fax: 630/990-0246
www.compassionatefriends.org
For parents whose child or children have died.

The Dougy Center
The National Center for Grieving Children and Families
P.O. Box 86852
Portland, OR 97286
Phone: 503/775-5683
Fax: 503/777-3097
www.dougy.org
For grieving children, teens, and families.

Fernside
A Center for Grieving Children
2303 Indian Mound Avenue
Cincinnati, OH 45212
Phone: 513/841-1012
Fax: 513/841-1546
www.fernside.org
For grieving children and their parents or guardians.

For the Love of Christi
2306 Hancock Drive
Austin, TX 78756
Phone: 512/467-2600
Fax: 512/467-2405
E-mail: for_love_christi@yahoo.com
www.forlovechristi.org
For anyone who is dealing with grief. Includes a special children's program and children's camp.

The Warm Place
1510 Cooper Street
Fort Worth, TX 76104-2710
Phone: 817/870-2272
Fax: 817/870-2570
E-mail: info@thewarmplace.org
www.thewarmplace.org
Grief support for children ages three to eighteen and their families.

Ferncliff Camp and Conference Center
1720 Ferncliff Road
Little Rock, AR 72223
Phone: 501/821-3063
Fax: 501/821-3093
E-mail: ferncliff@juno.com
www.ferncliff.org
Sponsor organization for TOUCH (Teens Offering Understanding, Caring, Healing), a national program that connects children affected by violence.

Other Web Sites to Visit for Advice

www.beliefnet.org Visit the Grief and Loss section of Family and Life Events. Articles, columns, discussions on all aspects of grief.

www.childrensgrief.net Linda Goldman—teacher, guidance counselor, author, certified grief therapist, and educator—offers advice on helping children through grief. Special sections on complicated grief.

www.saintsusanna.org The parish Web site of St. Susanna Church in Dedham, Massachusetts. Includes a section on bereavement books, videos, and workshops by pastor Father Terence Curley.

www.kidsaid.com Part of GriefNet, this site offers frequently asked questions for children and adults, poetry, stories, and a "kid-to-kid" support network.

www.kidsource.com/SIDS/index.html SIDS Foundation of Washington provides a chart listing the development concerns of children in grief as well as related articles.

www.hospicefoundation.org Hospice provides more than care for the terminally ill. This site offers "Living With Grief: Children, Adolescents, and Loss," a section that features basic information, books and videos for purchase, and an extensive list of links and resource organizations.

www.drgreene.com Pediatrician Alan Greene answers parents' questions about grief and other parenting issues.

www.centerforloss.com Site of the Center for Loss and Life Transition, run by renowned grief expert Dr. Alan Wolfelt.

NOTES

NOTES

NOTES

NOTES

NOTES

NOTES

APR - - 2002

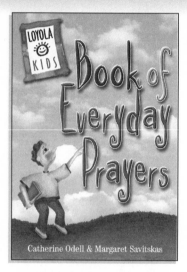